T0344746

THIS IS YOUR **PASSBOOK®** FOR ...

CLERK-TYPIST

NATIONAL LEARNING CORPORATION®
passbooks.com

COPYRIGHT NOTICE

Copyright © 2021 by

NLC®

National Learning Corporation

212 Michael Drive, Syosset, NY 11791
(516) 921-8888 • www.passbooks.com
E-mail: info@passbooks.com

PUBLISHED IN THE UNITED STATES OF AMERICA

PASSBOOK® SERIES

THE *PASSBOOK® SERIES* has been created to prepare applicants and candidates for the ultimate academic battlefield – the examination room.

At some time in our lives, each and every one of us may be required to take an examination – for validation, matriculation, admission, qualification, registration, certification, or licensure.

Based on the assumption that every applicant or candidate has met the basic formal educational standards, has taken the required number of courses, and read the necessary texts, the *PASSBOOK® SERIES* furnishes the one special preparation which may assure passing with confidence, instead of failing with insecurity. Examination questions – together with answers – are furnished as the basic vehicle for study so that the mysteries of the examination and its compounding difficulties may be eliminated or diminished by a sure method.

This book is meant to help you pass your examination provided that you qualify and are serious in your objective.

The entire field is reviewed through the huge store of content information which is succinctly presented through a provocative and challenging approach – the question-and-answer method.

A climate of success is established by furnishing the correct answers at the end of each test.

You soon learn to recognize types of questions, forms of questions, and patterns of questioning. You may even begin to anticipate expected outcomes.

You perceive that many questions are repeated or adapted so that you can gain acute insights, which may enable you to score many sure points.

You learn how to confront new questions, or types of questions, and to attack them confidently and work out the correct answers.

You note objectives and emphases, and recognize pitfalls and dangers, so that you may make positive educational adjustments.

Moreover, you are kept fully informed in relation to new concepts, methods, practices, and directions in the field.

You discover that you arre actually taking the examination all the time: you are preparing for the examination by "taking" an examination, not by reading extraneous and/or supererogatory textbooks.

In short, this PASSBOOK®, used directedly, should be an important factor in helping you to pass your test.

CLERK-TYPIST

DUTIES:

An employee in this class performs clerical and typing/word processing duties of limited difficulty and responsibility. The work of these positions, apart from typewriting, is similar in nature and level to that found in the clerk class. Duties of the position follow well-defined procedures and methods. Detailed instructions and close supervision are received at the beginning of work and on new assignments, but regular routine tasks are performed more independently and some initiative and judgment are utilized as experience is gained. The nature of the work is such that the employee may be required to operate a variety of office equipment. Employees may make arithmetical or other checks for accuracy of work performed by other employees, but they do not exercise direct supervision over other personnel. The work is performed under the direct supervision of assigned supervisory personnel, and is reviewed upon completion for content and accuracy. Does related work as required.

EXAMPLES OF WORK:

Types articles, forms, vendor's claims, letters, envelopes, memoranda, bulletins, reports, tabulations, purchase orders, cards, payrolls, trial calendar requisitions, marriage cards, copies of ordinances and resolutions, birth and death certificates and records, attendance and student records, case reports, commitment papers and other material using an alpha-numeric keyboard. Sorts and files correspondence; checks, vouchers, index cards or other materials, numerically, alphabetically or by other established classifications; sorts, dates stamps, distribute and/or deliver mail and packages; assists in the maintenance of personnel, payroll, equipment, or other records and in the preparation of reports; makes simple arithmetic calculations, computes data from requisitions, statistical reports, time reports or other records; occasionally may act as a receptionist and/or switchboard operator; operates standard office equipment including but not limited to photocopiers, fax machines, calculators, personal computers or computer terminals, and typewriters.

SUBJECTS OF THE EXAMINATION:

The written examination may test for knowledge, skills, and/or abilities in any of the following areas:

1. Spelling;
2. Alphabetizing;
3. Recordkeeping;
4. Clerical operations with letters and numbers;
5. Understanding and interpreting written material;
6. English usage; and
7. Proofreading.

HOW TO TAKE A TEST

I. YOU MUST PASS AN EXAMINATION

A. *WHAT EVERY CANDIDATE SHOULD KNOW*

Examination applicants often ask us for help in preparing for the written test. What can I study in advance? What kinds of questions will be asked? How will the test be given? How will the papers be graded?

As an applicant for a civil service examination, you may be wondering about some of these things. Our purpose here is to suggest effective methods of advance study and to describe civil service examinations.

Your chances for success on this examination can be increased if you know how to prepare. Those "pre-examination jitters" can be reduced if you know what to expect. You can even experience an adventure in good citizenship if you know why civil service exams are given.

B. *WHY ARE CIVIL SERVICE EXAMINATIONS GIVEN?*

Civil service examinations are important to you in two ways. As a citizen, you want public jobs filled by employees who know how to do their work. As a job seeker, you want a fair chance to compete for that job on an equal footing with other candidates. The best-known means of accomplishing this two-fold goal is the competitive examination.

Exams are widely publicized throughout the nation. They may be administered for jobs in federal, state, city, municipal, town or village governments or agencies.

Any citizen may apply, with some limitations, such as the age or residence of applicants. Your experience and education may be reviewed to see whether you meet the requirements for the particular examination. When these requirements exist, they are reasonable and applied consistently to all applicants. Thus, a competitive examination may cause you some uneasiness now, but it is your privilege and safeguard.

C. *HOW ARE CIVIL SERVICE EXAMS DEVELOPED?*

Examinations are carefully written by trained technicians who are specialists in the field known as "psychological measurement," in consultation with recognized authorities in the field of work that the test will cover. These experts recommend the subject matter areas or skills to be tested; only those knowledges or skills important to your success on the job are included. The most reliable books and source materials available are used as references. Together, the experts and technicians judge the difficulty level of the questions.

Test technicians know how to phrase questions so that the problem is clearly stated. Their ethics do not permit "trick" or "catch" questions. Questions may have been tried out on sample groups, or subjected to statistical analysis, to determine their usefulness.

Written tests are often used in combination with performance tests, ratings of training and experience, and oral interviews. All of these measures combine to form the best-known means of finding the right person for the right job.

II. HOW TO PASS THE WRITTEN TEST

A. *NATURE OF THE EXAMINATION*

To prepare intelligently for civil service examinations, you should know how they differ from school examinations you have taken. In school you were assigned certain definite pages to read or subjects to cover. The examination questions were quite detailed and usually emphasized memory. Civil service exams, on the other hand, try to discover your present ability to perform the duties of a position, plus your potentiality to learn these duties. In other words, a civil service exam attempts to predict how successful you will be. Questions cover such a broad area that they cannot be as minute and detailed as school exam questions.

In the public service similar kinds of work, or positions, are grouped together in one "class." This process is known as *position-classification*. All the positions in a class are paid according to the salary range for that class. One class title covers all of these positions, and they are all tested by the same examination.

B. *FOUR BASIC STEPS*

1) Study the announcement

How, then, can you know what subjects to study? Our best answer is: "Learn as much as possible about the class of positions for which you've applied." The exam will test the knowledge, skills and abilities needed to do the work.

Your most valuable source of information about the position you want is the official exam announcement. This announcement lists the training and experience qualifications. Check these standards and apply only if you come reasonably close to meeting them.

The brief description of the position in the examination announcement offers some clues to the subjects which will be tested. Think about the job itself. Review the duties in your mind. Can you perform them, or are there some in which you are rusty? Fill in the blank spots in your preparation.

Many jurisdictions preview the written test in the exam announcement by including a section called "Knowledge and Abilities Required," "Scope of the Examination," or some similar heading. Here you will find out specifically what fields will be tested.

2) Review your own background

Once you learn in general what the position is all about, and what you need to know to do the work, ask yourself which subjects you already know fairly well and which need improvement. You may wonder whether to concentrate on improving your strong areas or on building some background in your fields of weakness. When the announcement has specified "some knowledge" or "considerable knowledge," or has used adjectives like "beginning principles of…" or "advanced … methods," you can get a clue as to the number and difficulty of questions to be asked in any given field. More questions, and hence broader coverage, would be included for those subjects which are more important in the work. Now weigh your strengths and weaknesses against the job requirements and prepare accordingly.

3) Determine the level of the position

Another way to tell how intensively you should prepare is to understand the level of the job for which you are applying. Is it the entering level? In other words, is this the position in which beginners in a field of work are hired? Or is it an intermediate or advanced level? Sometimes this is indicated by such words as "Junior" or "Senior" in the class title. Other jurisdictions use Roman numerals to designate the level – Clerk I, Clerk II, for example. The word "Supervisor" sometimes appears in the title. If the level is not indicated by the title, check the description of duties. Will you be working under very close supervision, or will you have responsibility for independent decisions in this work?

4) Choose appropriate study materials

Now that you know the subjects to be examined and the relative amount of each subject to be covered, you can choose suitable study materials. For beginning level jobs, or even advanced ones, if you have a pronounced weakness in some aspect of your training, read a modern, standard textbook in that field. Be sure it is up to date and has general coverage. Such books are normally available at your library, and the librarian will be glad to help you locate one. For entry-level positions, questions of appropriate difficulty are chosen – neither highly advanced questions, nor those too simple. Such questions require careful thought but not advanced training.

If the position for which you are applying is technical or advanced, you will read more advanced, specialized material. If you are already familiar with the basic principles of your field, elementary textbooks would waste your time. Concentrate on advanced textbooks and technical periodicals. Think through the concepts and review difficult problems in your field.

These are all general sources. You can get more ideas on your own initiative, following these leads. For example, training manuals and publications of the government agency which employs workers in your field can be useful, particularly for technical and professional positions. A letter or visit to the government department involved may result in more specific study suggestions, and certainly will provide you with a more definite idea of the exact nature of the position you are seeking.

III. KINDS OF TESTS

Tests are used for purposes other than measuring knowledge and ability to perform specified duties. For some positions, it is equally important to test ability to make adjustments to new situations or to profit from training. In others, basic mental abilities not dependent on information are essential. Questions which test these things may not appear as pertinent to the duties of the position as those which test for knowledge and information. Yet they are often highly important parts of a fair examination. For very general questions, it is almost impossible to help you direct your study efforts. What we can do is to point out some of the more common of these general abilities needed in public service positions and describe some typical questions.

1) General information

Broad, general information has been found useful for predicting job success in some kinds of work. This is tested in a variety of ways, from vocabulary lists to questions about current events. Basic background in some field of work, such as sociology or economics, may be sampled in a group of questions. Often these are principles which have become familiar to most persons through exposure rather than through formal training. It is difficult to advise you how to study for these questions; being alert to the world around you is our best suggestion.

2) Verbal ability

An example of an ability needed in many positions is verbal or language ability. Verbal ability is, in brief, the ability to use and understand words. Vocabulary and grammar tests are typical measures of this ability. Reading comprehension or paragraph interpretation questions are common in many kinds of civil service tests. You are given a paragraph of written material and asked to find its central meaning.

3) Numerical ability

Number skills can be tested by the familiar arithmetic problem, by checking paired lists of numbers to see which are alike and which are different, or by interpreting charts and graphs. In the latter test, a graph may be printed in the test booklet which you are asked to use as the basis for answering questions.

4) Observation

A popular test for law-enforcement positions is the observation test. A picture is shown to you for several minutes, then taken away. Questions about the picture test your ability to observe both details and larger elements.

5) Following directions

In many positions in the public service, the employee must be able to carry out written instructions dependably and accurately. You may be given a chart with several columns, each column listing a variety of information. The questions require you to carry out directions involving the information given in the chart.

6) Skills and aptitudes

Performance tests effectively measure some manual skills and aptitudes. When the skill is one in which you are trained, such as typing or shorthand, you can practice. These tests are often very much like those given in business school or high school courses. For many of the other skills and aptitudes, however, no short-time preparation can be made. Skills and abilities natural to you or that you have developed throughout your lifetime are being tested.

Many of the general questions just described provide all the data needed to answer the questions and ask you to use your reasoning ability to find the answers. Your best preparation for these tests, as well as for tests of facts and ideas, is to be at your physical and mental best. You, no doubt, have your own methods of getting into an exam-taking mood and keeping "in shape." The next section lists some ideas on this subject.

IV. KINDS OF QUESTIONS

Only rarely is the "essay" question, which you answer in narrative form, used in civil service tests. Civil service tests are usually of the short-answer type. Full instructions for answering these questions will be given to you at the examination. But in case this is your first experience with short-answer questions and separate answer sheets, here is what you need to know:

1) Multiple-choice Questions

Most popular of the short-answer questions is the "multiple choice" or "best answer" question. It can be used, for example, to test for factual knowledge, ability to solve problems or judgment in meeting situations found at work.

A multiple-choice question is normally one of three types —

- It can begin with an incomplete statement followed by several possible endings. You are to find the one ending which *best* completes the statement, although some of the others may not be entirely wrong.
- It can also be a complete statement in the form of a question which is answered by choosing one of the statements listed.
- It can be in the form of a problem – again you select the best answer.

Here is an example of a multiple-choice question with a discussion which should give you some clues as to the method for choosing the right answer:

When an employee has a complaint about his assignment, the action which will *best* help him overcome his difficulty is to
A. discuss his difficulty with his coworkers
B. take the problem to the head of the organization
C. take the problem to the person who gave him the assignment
D. say nothing to anyone about his complaint

In answering this question, you should study each of the choices to find which is best. Consider choice "A" – Certainly an employee may discuss his complaint with fellow employees, but no change or improvement can result, and the complaint remains unresolved. Choice "B" is a poor choice since the head of the organization probably does not know what assignment you have been given, and taking your problem to him is known as "going over the head" of the supervisor. The supervisor, or person who made the assignment, is the person who can clarify it or correct any injustice. Choice "C" is, therefore, correct. To say nothing, as in choice "D," is unwise. Supervisors have and interest in knowing the problems employees are facing, and the employee is seeking a solution to his problem.

2) True/False Questions

The "true/false" or "right/wrong" form of question is sometimes used. Here a complete statement is given. Your job is to decide whether the statement is right or wrong.

SAMPLE: A roaming cell-phone call to a nearby city costs less than a non-roaming call to a distant city.

This statement is wrong, or false, since roaming calls are more expensive.
This is not a complete list of all possible question forms, although most of the others are variations of these common types. You will always get complete directions for

answering questions. Be sure you understand *how* to mark your answers – ask questions until you do.

V. RECORDING YOUR ANSWERS

Computer terminals are used more and more today for many different kinds of exams.

For an examination with very few applicants, you may be told to record your answers in the test booklet itself. Separate answer sheets are much more common. If this separate answer sheet is to be scored by machine – and this is often the case – it is highly important that you mark your answers correctly in order to get credit.

An electronic scoring machine is often used in civil service offices because of the speed with which papers can be scored. Machine-scored answer sheets must be marked with a pencil, which will be given to you. This pencil has a high graphite content which responds to the electronic scoring machine. As a matter of fact, stray dots may register as answers, so do not let your pencil rest on the answer sheet while you are pondering the correct answer. Also, if your pencil lead breaks or is otherwise defective, ask for another.

Since the answer sheet will be dropped in a slot in the scoring machine, be careful not to bend the corners or get the paper crumpled.

The answer sheet normally has five vertical columns of numbers, with 30 numbers to a column. These numbers correspond to the question numbers in your test booklet. After each number, going across the page are four or five pairs of dotted lines. These short dotted lines have small letters or numbers above them. The first two pairs may also have a "T" or "F" above the letters. This indicates that the first two pairs only are to be used if the questions are of the true-false type. If the questions are multiple choice, disregard the "T" and "F" and pay attention only to the small letters or numbers.

Answer your questions in the manner of the sample that follows:

32. The largest city in the United States is
    A. Washington, D.C.
    B. New York City
    C. Chicago
    D. Detroit
    E. San Francisco

1) Choose the answer you think is best. (New York City is the largest, so "B" is correct.)
2) Find the row of dotted lines numbered the same as the question you are answering. (Find row number 32)
3) Find the pair of dotted lines corresponding to the answer. (Find the pair of lines under the mark "B.")
4) Make a solid black mark between the dotted lines.

VI. BEFORE THE TEST

Common sense will help you find procedures to follow to get ready for an examination. Too many of us, however, overlook these sensible measures. Indeed, nervousness and fatigue have been found to be the most serious reasons why applicants fail to do their best on civil service tests. Here is a list of reminders:

- Begin your preparation early – Don't wait until the last minute to go scurrying around for books and materials or to find out what the position is all about.
- Prepare continuously – An hour a night for a week is better than an all-night cram session. This has been definitely established. What is more, a night a week for a month will return better dividends than crowding your study into a shorter period of time.
- Locate the place of the exam – You have been sent a notice telling you when and where to report for the examination. If the location is in a different town or otherwise unfamiliar to you, it would be well to inquire the best route and learn something about the building.
- Relax the night before the test – Allow your mind to rest. Do not study at all that night. Plan some mild recreation or diversion; then go to bed early and get a good night's sleep.
- Get up early enough to make a leisurely trip to the place for the test – This way unforeseen events, traffic snarls, unfamiliar buildings, etc. will not upset you.
- Dress comfortably – A written test is not a fashion show. You will be known by number and not by name, so wear something comfortable.
- Leave excess paraphernalia at home – Shopping bags and odd bundles will get in your way. You need bring only the items mentioned in the official notice you received; usually everything you need is provided. Do not bring reference books to the exam. They will only confuse those last minutes and be taken away from you when in the test room.
- Arrive somewhat ahead of time – If because of transportation schedules you must get there very early, bring a newspaper or magazine to take your mind off yourself while waiting.
- Locate the examination room – When you have found the proper room, you will be directed to the seat or part of the room where you will sit. Sometimes you are given a sheet of instructions to read while you are waiting. Do not fill out any forms until you are told to do so; just read them and be prepared.
- Relax and prepare to listen to the instructions
- If you have any physical problem that may keep you from doing your best, be sure to tell the test administrator. If you are sick or in poor health, you really cannot do your best on the exam. You can come back and take the test some other time.

VII. AT THE TEST

The day of the test is here and you have the test booklet in your hand. The temptation to get going is very strong. Caution! There is more to success than knowing the right answers. You must know how to identify your papers and understand variations in the type of short-answer question used in this particular examination. Follow these suggestions for maximum results from your efforts:

1) Cooperate with the monitor

The test administrator has a duty to create a situation in which you can be as much at ease as possible. He will give instructions, tell you when to begin, check to see that you are marking your answer sheet correctly, and so on. He is not there to guard you, although he will see that your competitors do not take unfair advantage. He wants to help you do your best.

2) Listen to all instructions

Don't jump the gun! Wait until you understand all directions. In most civil service tests you get more time than you need to answer the questions. So don't be in a hurry. Read each word of instructions until you clearly understand the meaning. Study the examples, listen to all announcements and follow directions. Ask questions if you do not understand what to do.

3) Identify your papers

Civil service exams are usually identified by number only. You will be assigned a number; you must not put your name on your test papers. Be sure to copy your number correctly. Since more than one exam may be given, copy your exact examination title.

4) Plan your time

Unless you are told that a test is a "speed" or "rate of work" test, speed itself is usually not important. Time enough to answer all the questions will be provided, but this does not mean that you have all day. An overall time limit has been set. Divide the total time (in minutes) by the number of questions to determine the approximate time you have for each question.

5) Do not linger over difficult questions

If you come across a difficult question, mark it with a paper clip (useful to have along) and come back to it when you have been through the booklet. One caution if you do this – be sure to skip a number on your answer sheet as well. Check often to be sure that you have not lost your place and that you are marking in the row numbered the same as the question you are answering.

6) Read the questions

Be sure you know what the question asks! Many capable people are unsuccessful because they failed to *read* the questions correctly.

7) Answer all questions

Unless you have been instructed that a penalty will be deducted for incorrect answers, it is better to guess than to omit a question.

8) Speed tests

It is often better NOT to guess on speed tests. It has been found that on timed tests people are tempted to spend the last few seconds before time is called in marking answers at random – without even reading them – in the hope of picking up a few extra points. To discourage this practice, the instructions may warn you that your score will be "corrected" for guessing. That is, a penalty will be applied. The incorrect answers will be deducted from the correct ones, or some other penalty formula will be used.

9) Review your answers

If you finish before time is called, go back to the questions you guessed or omitted to give them further thought. Review other answers if you have time.

10) Return your test materials

If you are ready to leave before others have finished or time is called, take ALL your materials to the monitor and leave quietly. Never take any test material with you. The monitor can discover whose papers are not complete, and taking a test booklet may be grounds for disqualification.

VIII. EXAMINATION TECHNIQUES

1) Read the general instructions carefully. These are usually printed on the first page of the exam booklet. As a rule, these instructions refer to the timing of the examination; the fact that you should not start work until the signal and must stop work at a signal, etc. If there are any *special* instructions, such as a choice of questions to be answered, make sure that you note this instruction carefully.

2) When you are ready to start work on the examination, that is as soon as the signal has been given, read the instructions to each question booklet, underline any key words or phrases, such as *least, best, outline, describe* and the like. In this way you will tend to answer as requested rather than discover on reviewing your paper that you *listed without describing*, that you selected the *worst* choice rather than the *best* choice, etc.

3) If the examination is of the objective or multiple-choice type – that is, each question will also give a series of possible answers: A, B, C or D, and you are called upon to select the best answer and write the letter next to that answer on your answer paper – it is advisable to start answering each question in turn. There may be anywhere from 50 to 100 such questions in the three or four hours allotted and you can see how much time would be taken if you read through all the questions before beginning to answer any. Furthermore, if you come across a question or group of questions which you know would be difficult to answer, it would undoubtedly affect your handling of all the other questions.

4) If the examination is of the essay type and contains but a few questions, it is a moot point as to whether you should read all the questions before starting to answer any one. Of course, if you are given a choice – say five out of seven and the like – then it is essential to read all the questions so you can eliminate the two that are most difficult. If, however, you are asked to answer all the questions, there may be danger in trying to answer the easiest one first because you may find that you will spend too much time on it. The best technique is to answer the first question, then proceed to the second, etc.

5) Time your answers. Before the exam begins, write down the time it started, then add the time allowed for the examination and write down the time it must be completed, then divide the time available somewhat as follows:

- If 3-1/2 hours are allowed, that would be 210 minutes. If you have 80 objective-type questions, that would be an average of 2-1/2 minutes per question. Allow yourself no more than 2 minutes per question, or a total of 160 minutes, which will permit about 50 minutes to review.
- If for the time allotment of 210 minutes there are 7 essay questions to answer, that would average about 30 minutes a question. Give yourself only 25 minutes per question so that you have about 35 minutes to review.

6) The most important instruction is to *read each question* and make sure you know what is wanted. The second most important instruction is to *time yourself properly* so that you answer every question. The third most important instruction is to *answer every question*. Guess if you have to but include something for each question. Remember that you will receive no credit for a blank and will probably receive some credit if you write something in answer to an essay question. If you guess a letter – say "B" for a multiple-choice question – you may have guessed right. If you leave a blank as an answer to a multiple-choice question, the examiners may respect your feelings but it will not add a point to your score. Some exams may penalize you for wrong answers, so in such cases *only*, you may not want to guess unless you have some basis for your answer.

7) Suggestions
   a. Objective-type questions
      1. Examine the question booklet for proper sequence of pages and questions
      2. Read all instructions carefully
      3. Skip any question which seems too difficult; return to it after all other questions have been answered
      4. Apportion your time properly; do not spend too much time on any single question or group of questions
      5. Note and underline key words – *all, most, fewest, least, best, worst, same, opposite,* etc.
      6. Pay particular attention to negatives
      7. Note unusual option, e.g., unduly long, short, complex, different or similar in content to the body of the question
      8. Observe the use of "hedging" words – *probably, may, most likely,* etc.
      9. Make sure that your answer is put next to the same number as the question
      10. Do not second-guess unless you have good reason to believe the second answer is definitely more correct
      11. Cross out original answer if you decide another answer is more accurate; do not erase until you are ready to hand your paper in
      12. Answer all questions; guess unless instructed otherwise
      13. Leave time for review

   b. Essay questions
      1. Read each question carefully
      2. Determine exactly what is wanted. Underline key words or phrases.
      3. Decide on outline or paragraph answer

4. Include many different points and elements unless asked to develop any one or two points or elements
5. Show impartiality by giving pros and cons unless directed to select one side only
6. Make and write down any assumptions you find necessary to answer the questions
7. Watch your English, grammar, punctuation and choice of words
8. Time your answers; don't crowd material

8) Answering the essay question

Most essay questions can be answered by framing the specific response around several key words or ideas. Here are a few such key words or ideas:

M's: manpower, materials, methods, money, management
P's: purpose, program, policy, plan, procedure, practice, problems, pitfalls, personnel, public relations
   a. Six basic steps in handling problems:
      1. Preliminary plan and background development
      2. Collect information, data and facts
      3. Analyze and interpret information, data and facts
      4. Analyze and develop solutions as well as make recommendations
      5. Prepare report and sell recommendations
      6. Install recommendations and follow up effectiveness

   b. Pitfalls to avoid
      1. *Taking things for granted* – A statement of the situation does not necessarily imply that each of the elements is necessarily true; for example, a complaint may be invalid and biased so that all that can be taken for granted is that a complaint has been registered
      2. *Considering only one side of a situation* – Wherever possible, indicate several alternatives and then point out the reasons you selected the best one
      3. *Failing to indicate follow up* – Whenever your answer indicates action on your part, make certain that you will take proper follow-up action to see how successful your recommendations, procedures or actions turn out to be
      4. *Taking too long in answering any single question* – Remember to time your answers properly

IX. AFTER THE TEST

Scoring procedures differ in detail among civil service jurisdictions although the general principles are the same. Whether the papers are hand-scored or graded by machine we have described, they are nearly always graded by number. That is, the person who marks the paper knows only the number – never the name – of the applicant. Not until all the papers have been graded will they be matched with names. If other tests, such as training and experience or oral interview ratings have been given, scores will be combined. Different parts of the examination usually have different weights. For example, the written test might count 60 percent of the final grade, and a rating of training and experience 40 percent. In many jurisdictions, veterans will have a certain number of points added to their grades.

After the final grade has been determined, the names are placed in grade order and an eligible list is established. There are various methods for resolving ties between those who get the same final grade – probably the most common is to place first the name of the person whose application was received first. Job offers are made from the eligible list in the order the names appear on it. You will be notified of your grade and your rank as soon as all these computations have been made. This will be done as rapidly as possible.

People who are found to meet the requirements in the announcement are called "eligibles." Their names are put on a list of eligible candidates. An eligible's chances of getting a job depend on how high he stands on this list and how fast agencies are filling jobs from the list.

When a job is to be filled from a list of eligibles, the agency asks for the names of people on the list of eligibles for that job. When the civil service commission receives this request, it sends to the agency the names of the three people highest on this list. Or, if the job to be filled has specialized requirements, the office sends the agency the names of the top three persons who meet these requirements from the general list.

The appointing officer makes a choice from among the three people whose names were sent to him. If the selected person accepts the appointment, the names of the others are put back on the list to be considered for future openings.

That is the rule in hiring from all kinds of eligible lists, whether they are for typist, carpenter, chemist, or something else. For every vacancy, the appointing officer has his choice of any one of the top three eligibles on the list. This explains why the person whose name is on top of the list sometimes does not get an appointment when some of the persons lower on the list do. If the appointing officer chooses the second or third eligible, the No. 1 eligible does not get a job at once, but stays on the list until he is appointed or the list is terminated.

X. HOW TO PASS THE INTERVIEW TEST

The examination for which you applied requires an oral interview test. You have already taken the written test and you are now being called for the interview test – the final part of the formal examination.

You may think that it is not possible to prepare for an interview test and that there are no procedures to follow during an interview. Our purpose is to point out some things you can do in advance that will help you and some good rules to follow and pitfalls to avoid while you are being interviewed.

What is an interview supposed to test?
The written examination is designed to test the technical knowledge and competence of the candidate; the oral is designed to evaluate intangible qualities, not readily measured otherwise, and to establish a list showing the relative fitness of each candidate – as measured against his competitors – for the position sought. Scoring is not on the basis of "right" and "wrong," but on a sliding scale of values ranging from "not passable" to "outstanding." As a matter of fact, it is possible to achieve a relatively low score without a single "incorrect" answer because of evident weakness in the qualities being measured.

Occasionally, an examination may consist entirely of an oral test – either an individual or a group oral. In such cases, information is sought concerning the technical knowledges and abilities of the candidate, since there has been no written examination for this purpose. More commonly, however, an oral test is used to supplement a written examination.

Who conducts interviews?

The composition of oral boards varies among different jurisdictions. In nearly all, a representative of the personnel department serves as chairman. One of the members of the board may be a representative of the department in which the candidate would work. In some cases, "outside experts" are used, and, frequently, a businessman or some other representative of the general public is asked to serve. Labor and management or other special groups may be represented. The aim is to secure the services of experts in the appropriate field.

However the board is composed, it is a good idea (and not at all improper or unethical) to ascertain in advance of the interview who the members are and what groups they represent. When you are introduced to them, you will have some idea of their backgrounds and interests, and at least you will not stutter and stammer over their names.

What should be done before the interview?

While knowledge about the board members is useful and takes some of the surprise element out of the interview, there is other preparation which is more substantive. It *is* possible to prepare for an oral interview – in several ways:

1) Keep a copy of your application and review it carefully before the interview

This may be the only document before the oral board, and the starting point of the interview. Know what education and experience you have listed there, and the sequence and dates of all of it. Sometimes the board will ask you to review the highlights of your experience for them; you should not have to hem and haw doing it.

2) Study the class specification and the examination announcement

Usually, the oral board has one or both of these to guide them. The qualities, characteristics or knowledges required by the position sought are stated in these documents. They offer valuable clues as to the nature of the oral interview. For example, if the job involves supervisory responsibilities, the announcement will usually indicate that knowledge of modern supervisory methods and the qualifications of the candidate as a supervisor will be tested. If so, you can expect such questions, frequently in the form of a hypothetical situation which you are expected to solve. NEVER go into an oral without knowledge of the duties and responsibilities of the job you seek.

3) Think through each qualification required

Try to visualize the kind of questions you would ask if you were a board member. How well could you answer them? Try especially to appraise your own knowledge and background in each area, *measured against the job sought*, and identify any areas in which you are weak. Be critical and realistic – do not flatter yourself.

4) Do some general reading in areas in which you feel you may be weak

For example, if the job involves supervision and your past experience has NOT, some general reading in supervisory methods and practices, particularly in the field of human relations, might be useful. Do NOT study agency procedures or detailed manuals. The oral board will be testing your understanding and capacity, not your memory.

5) Get a good night's sleep and watch your general health and mental attitude

You will want a clear head at the interview. Take care of a cold or any other minor ailment, and of course, no hangovers.

What should be done on the day of the interview?

Now comes the day of the interview itself. Give yourself plenty of time to get there. Plan to arrive somewhat ahead of the scheduled time, particularly if your appointment is in the fore part of the day. If a previous candidate fails to appear, the board might be ready for you a bit early. By early afternoon an oral board is almost invariably behind schedule if there are many candidates, and you may have to wait. Take along a book or magazine to read, or your application to review, but leave any extraneous material in the waiting room when you go in for your interview. In any event, relax and compose yourself.

The matter of dress is important. The board is forming impressions about you – from your experience, your manners, your attitude, and your appearance. Give your personal appearance careful attention. Dress your best, but not your flashiest. Choose conservative, appropriate clothing, and be sure it is immaculate. This is a business interview, and your appearance should indicate that you regard it as such. Besides, being well groomed and properly dressed will help boost your confidence.

Sooner or later, someone will call your name and escort you into the interview room. *This is it.* From here on you are on your own. It is too late for any more preparation. But remember, you asked for this opportunity to prove your fitness, and you are here because your request was granted.

What happens when you go in?

The usual sequence of events will be as follows: The clerk (who is often the board stenographer) will introduce you to the chairman of the oral board, who will introduce you to the other members of the board. Acknowledge the introductions before you sit down. Do not be surprised if you find a microphone facing you or a stenotypist sitting by. Oral interviews are usually recorded in the event of an appeal or other review.

Usually the chairman of the board will open the interview by reviewing the highlights of your education and work experience from your application – primarily for the benefit of the other members of the board, as well as to get the material into the record. Do not interrupt or comment unless there is an error or significant misinterpretation; if that is the case, do not hesitate. But do not quibble about insignificant matters. Also, he will usually ask you some question about your education, experience or your present job – partly to get you to start talking and to establish the interviewing "rapport." He may start the actual questioning, or turn it over to one of the other members. Frequently, each member undertakes the questioning on a particular area, one in which he is perhaps most competent, so you can expect each member to participate in the examination. Because time is limited, you may also expect some rather abrupt switches in the direction the questioning takes, so do not be upset by it. Normally, a board member will not pursue a single line of questioning unless he discovers a particular strength or weakness.

After each member has participated, the chairman will usually ask whether any member has any further questions, then will ask you if you have anything you wish to add. Unless you are expecting this question, it may floor you. Worse, it may start you off on an extended, extemporaneous speech. The board is not usually seeking more information. The question is principally to offer you a last opportunity to present further qualifications or to indicate that you have nothing to add. So, if you feel that a significant qualification or characteristic has been overlooked, it is proper to point it out in a sentence or so. Do not compliment the board on the thoroughness of their examination – they have been sketchy, and you know it. If you wish, merely say, "No thank you, I have nothing further to add." This is a point where you can "talk yourself out" of a good impression or fail to present an important bit of information. Remember, *you close the interview yourself.*

The chairman will then say, "That is all, Mr. _____, thank you." Do not be startled; the interview is over, and quicker than you think. Thank him, gather your belongings and take your leave. Save your sigh of relief for the other side of the door.

How to put your best foot forward
Throughout this entire process, you may feel that the board individually and collectively is trying to pierce your defenses, seek out your hidden weaknesses and embarrass and confuse you. Actually, this is not true. They are obliged to make an appraisal of your qualifications for the job you are seeking, and they want to see you in your best light. Remember, they must interview all candidates and a non-cooperative candidate may become a failure in spite of their best efforts to bring out his qualifications. Here are 15 suggestions that will help you:

1) Be natural – Keep your attitude confident, not cocky
If you are not confident that you can do the job, do not expect the board to be. Do not apologize for your weaknesses, try to bring out your strong points. The board is interested in a positive, not negative, presentation. Cockiness will antagonize any board member and make him wonder if you are covering up a weakness by a false show of strength.

2) Get comfortable, but don't lounge or sprawl
Sit erectly but not stiffly. A careless posture may lead the board to conclude that you are careless in other things, or at least that you are not impressed by the importance of the occasion. Either conclusion is natural, even if incorrect. Do not fuss with your clothing, a pencil or an ashtray. Your hands may occasionally be useful to emphasize a point; do not let them become a point of distraction.

3) Do not wisecrack or make small talk
This is a serious situation, and your attitude should show that you consider it as such. Further, the time of the board is limited – they do not want to waste it, and neither should you.

4) Do not exaggerate your experience or abilities
In the first place, from information in the application or other interviews and sources, the board may know more about you than you think. Secondly, you probably will not get away with it. An experienced board is rather adept at spotting such a situation, so do not take the chance.

5) If you know a board member, do not make a point of it, yet do not hide it

Certainly you are not fooling him, and probably not the other members of the board. Do not try to take advantage of your acquaintanceship – it will probably do you little good.

6) Do not dominate the interview

Let the board do that. They will give you the clues – do not assume that you have to do all the talking. Realize that the board has a number of questions to ask you, and do not try to take up all the interview time by showing off your extensive knowledge of the answer to the first one.

7) Be attentive

You only have 20 minutes or so, and you should keep your attention at its sharpest throughout. When a member is addressing a problem or question to you, give him your undivided attention. Address your reply principally to him, but do not exclude the other board members.

8) Do not interrupt

A board member may be stating a problem for you to analyze. He will ask you a question when the time comes. Let him state the problem, and wait for the question.

9) Make sure you understand the question

Do not try to answer until you are sure what the question is. If it is not clear, restate it in your own words or ask the board member to clarify it for you. However, do not haggle about minor elements.

10) Reply promptly but not hastily

A common entry on oral board rating sheets is "candidate responded readily," or "candidate hesitated in replies." Respond as promptly and quickly as you can, but do not jump to a hasty, ill-considered answer.

11) Do not be peremptory in your answers

A brief answer is proper – but do not fire your answer back. That is a losing game from your point of view. The board member can probably ask questions much faster than you can answer them.

12) Do not try to create the answer you think the board member wants

He is interested in what kind of mind you have and how it works – not in playing games. Furthermore, he can usually spot this practice and will actually grade you down on it.

13) Do not switch sides in your reply merely to agree with a board member

Frequently, a member will take a contrary position merely to draw you out and to see if you are willing and able to defend your point of view. Do not start a debate, yet do not surrender a good position. If a position is worth taking, it is worth defending.

14) Do not be afraid to admit an error in judgment if you are shown to be wrong

The board knows that you are forced to reply without any opportunity for careful consideration. Your answer may be demonstrably wrong. If so, admit it and get on with the interview.

15) Do not dwell at length on your present job

The opening question may relate to your present assignment. Answer the question but do not go into an extended discussion. You are being examined for a *new* job, not your present one. As a matter of fact, try to phrase ALL your answers in terms of the job for which you are being examined.

Basis of Rating

Probably you will forget most of these "do's" and "don'ts" when you walk into the oral interview room. Even remembering them all will not ensure you a passing grade. Perhaps you did not have the qualifications in the first place. But remembering them will help you to put your best foot forward, without treading on the toes of the board members.

Rumor and popular opinion to the contrary notwithstanding, an oral board wants you to make the best appearance possible. They know you are under pressure – but they also want to see how you respond to it as a guide to what your reaction would be under the pressures of the job you seek. They will be influenced by the degree of poise you display, the personal traits you show and the manner in which you respond.

ABOUT THIS BOOK

This book contains tests divided into Examination Sections. Go through each test, answering every question in the margin. At the end of each test look at the answer key and check your answers. On the ones you got wrong, look at the right answer choice and learn. Do not fill in the answers first. Do not memorize the questions and answers, but understand the answer and principles involved. On your test, the questions will likely be different from the samples. Questions are changed and new ones added. If you understand these past questions you should have success with any changes that arise. Tests may consist of several types of questions. We have additional books on each subject should more study be advisable or necessary for you. Finally, the more you study, the better prepared you will be. This book is intended to be the last thing you study before you walk into the examination room. Prior study of relevant texts is also recommended. NLC publishes some of these in our Fundamental Series. Knowledge and good sense are important factors in passing your exam. Good luck also helps. So now study this Passbook, absorb the material contained within and take that knowledge into the examination. Then do your best to pass that exam.

EXAMINATION SECTION

EXAMINATION SECTION
TEST 1

DIRECTIONS: Each question or incomplete statement is followed by several suggested answers or completions. Select the one that BEST answers the question or completes the statement. *PRINT THE LETTER OF THE CORRECT ANSWER IN THE SPACE AT THE RIGHT.*

1. Assume that a few co-workers meet near your desk and talk about personal matters during working hours. Lately, this practice has interfered with your work.
   In order to stop this practice, the BEST action for you to take FIRST is to

   A. ask your supervisor to put a stop to the co-workers' meeting near your desk
   B. discontinue any friendship with this group
   C. ask your co-workers not to meet near your desk
   D. request that your desk be moved to another location

   1.____

2. In order to maintain office coverage during working hours, your supervisor has scheduled your lunch hour from 1 P.M. to 2 P.M. and your co-worker's lunch hour from 12 P.M. to 1 P.M. Lately, your co-worker has been returning late from lunch each day. As a result, you don't get a full hour since you must return to the office by 2 P.M.
   Of the following, the BEST action for you to take FIRST is to

   A. explain to your co-worker in a courteous manner that his lateness is interfering with your right to a full hour for lunch
   B. tell your co-worker that his lateness must stop or you will report him to your supervisor
   C. report your co-worker's lateness to your supervisor
   D. leave at 1 P.M. for lunch, whether your co-worker has returned or not

   2.____

3. Assume that, as an office worker, one of your jobs is to open mail sent to your unit, read the mail for content, and send the mail to the appropriate person to handle. You accidentally open and begin to read a letter marked *personal* addressed to a co-worker.
   Of the following, the BEST action for you to take is to

   A. report to your supervisor that your co-worker is receiving personal mail at the office
   B. destroy the letter so that your co-worker does not know you saw it
   C. reseal the letter and place it on the co-worker's desk without saying anything
   D. bring the letter to your co-worker and explain that you opened it by accident

   3.____

4. Suppose that in evaluating your work, your supervisor gives you an overall good rating, but states that you sometimes turn in work with careless errors.
   The BEST action for you to take would be to

   A. ask a co-worker who is good at details to proofread your work
   B. take time to do a careful job, paying more attention to detail
   C. continue working as usual since occasional errors are to be expected
   D. ask your supervisor if she would mind correcting your errors

   4.____

5. Assume that you are taking a telephone message for a co-worker who is not in the office at the time.
   Of the following, the LEAST important item to write on the message is the

   A. length of the call
   B. name of the caller
   C. time of the call
   D. telephone number of the caller

   5.____

Questions 6-13.

DIRECTIONS: Questions 6 through 13 each consist of a sentence which may or may not be an example of good English. The underlined parts of each sentence may be correct or incorrect. Examine each sentence, considering grammar, punctuation, spelling, and capitalization. If the English usage in the underlined parts of the sentence given is better than any of the changes in the underlined words suggested in Options B, C, or D, choose Option A. If the changes in the underlined words suggested in Options B, C, or D would make the sentence correct, choose the correct option. Do not choose an option that will change the meaning of the sentence.

6. This <u>Fall</u>, the office will be closed on <u>Columbus Day</u>, <u>October</u> 9th.   6.____

    A. Correct as is
    B. fall...Columbus Day, October
    C. Fall...columbus day, October
    D. fall...Columbus Day, october

7. This manual <u>discribes the duties performed</u> by an Office Aide.   7.____

    A. Correct as is
    B. describe the duties performed
    C. discribe the duties performed
    D. describes the duties performed

8. There <u>weren't no</u> paper in the supply closet.   8.____

    A. Correct as is   B. weren't any
    C. wasn't any   D. wasn't no

9. The new employees left <u>there</u> office to attend a meeting.   9.____

    A. Correct as is   B. they're
    C. their   D. thier

10. The office worker started working at <u>8;30 a.m.</u>   10.____

    A. Correct as is   B. 8:30 a.m.
    C. 8;30 a,m.   D. 8:30 am

11. The <u>alphabet, or A to Z sequence</u> are the basis of most filing systems.   11.____

    A. Correct as is
    B. alphabet, or A to Z sequence, is
    C. alphabet, or A to Z sequence are
    D. alphabet, or A too Z sequence, is

12. <u>Those</u> file cabinets are five <u>feet</u> tall.   12.____

    A. Correct as is   B. Them...feet
    C. Those...foot   D. Them...foot

13. The Office Aide checked the <u>register and finding</u> the date of the meeting.   13._____

    A. Correct as is   B. regaster and finding
    C. register and found   D. regaster and found

Questions 14-21.

DIRECTIONS: Each of Questions 14 through 21 has two lists of numbers. Each list contains three sets of numbers. Check each of the three sets in the list on the right to see if they are the same as the corresponding set in the list on the left. Mark your answers:

    A. If none of the sets in the right list are the same as those in the left list
    B. if only one of the sets in the right list are the same as those in the left list
    C. if only two of the sets in the right list are the same as those in the left list
    D. if all three sets in the right list are the same as those in the left list

14. 7354183476   7354983476   14._____
     4474747744   4474747774
     57914302311   57914302311

15. 7143592185   7143892185   15._____
     8344517699   8344518699
     9178531263   9178531263

16. 2572114731   257214731   16._____
     8806835476   8806835476
     8255831246   8255831246

17. 331476853821   331476858621   17._____
     6976658532996   6976655832996
     3766042113715   3766042113745

18. 8806663315   8806663315   18._____
     74477138449   74477138449
     211756663666   211756663666

19. 990006966996   99000696996   19._____
     53022219743   53022219843
     4171171117717   4171171177717

20. 24400222433004   24400222433004   20._____
     5300030055000355   5300030055500355
     20000075532002022   20000075532002022

21. 61116664066001116   61116664066001116   21._____
     7111300117001100733   7111300117001100733
     26666446664476518   26666446664476518

3

Questions 22-25.

DIRECTIONS: Each of Questions 22 through 25 has two lists of names and addresses. Each list contains three sets of names and addresses. Check each of the three sets in the list on the right to see if they are the same as the corresponding set in the list on the left. Mark your answers:

    A.   if none of the sets in the right list are the same as those in the left list

    B.   if only one of the sets in the right list is the same as those in the left list

    C.   if only two of the sets in the right list are the same as those in the left list

    D.   if all three sets in the right list are the same as those in the left list

22.   Mary T. Berlinger
2351 Hampton St.
Monsey, N.Y. 20117

Eduardo Benes
473 Kingston Avenue
Central Islip, N.Y. 11734

Alan Carrington Fuchs
17 Gnarled Hollow Road
Los Angeles, CA 91635

   Mary T. Berlinger
2351 Hampton St.
Monsey, N.Y. 20117

Eduardo Benes
473 Kingston Avenue
Central Islip, N.Y. 11734

Alan Carrington Fuchs
17 Gnarled Hollow Road
Los Angeles, CA 91685

22.____

23.   David John Jacobson
178 35 St. Apt. 4C
New York, N.Y. 00927

Ann-Marie Calonella
7243 South Ridge Blvd.
Bakersfield, CA 96714

Pauline M. Thompson
872 Linden Ave.
Houston, Texas 70321

   David John Jacobson
178 53 St. Apt. 4C
New York, N.Y. 00927

Ann-Marie Calonella
7243 South Ridge Blvd.
Bakersfield, CA 96714

Pauline M. Thomson
872 Linden Ave.
Houston, Texas 70321

23.____

24.   Chester LeRoy Masterton
152 Lacy Rd.
Kankakee, Ill. 54532

William Maloney
S. LaCrosse Pla.
Wausau, Wisconsin 52146

Cynthia V. Barnes
16 Pines Rd.
Greenpoint, Miss. 20376

   Chester LeRoy Masterson
152 Lacy Rd.
Kankakee, Ill. 54532

William Maloney
S. LaCross Pla.
Wausau, Wisconsin 52146

Cynthia V. Barnes
16 Pines Rd.
Greenpoint, Miss. 20376

24.____

25.   Marcel Jean Frontenac   Marcel Jean Frontenac   25.____
     6 Burton On The Water   6 Burton On The Water
     Calender, Me. 01471   Calender, Me. 01471

     J. Scott Marsden   J. Scott Marsden
     174 S. Tipton St.   174 Tipton St.
     Cleveland, Ohio   Cleveland, Ohio

     Lawrence T. Haney   Lawrence T. Haney
     171 McDonough St.   171 McDonough St.
     Decatur, Ga. 31304   Decatur, Ga. 31304

KEY (CORRECT ANSWERS)

1.	C		11.	B
2.	A		12.	A
3.	D		13.	C
4.	B		14.	B
5.	A		15.	B
6.	A		16.	C
7.	D		17.	A
8.	C		18.	D
9.	C		19.	A
10.	B		20.	C

21.	C
22.	C
23.	B
24.	B
25.	C

TEST 2

DIRECTIONS: Each question or incomplete statement is followed by several suggested answers or completions. Select the one that BEST answers the question or completes the statement. *PRINT THE LETTER OF THE CORRECT ANSWER IN THE SPACE AT THE RIGHT.*

Questions 1-6.

DIRECTIONS: Questions 1 through 6 are to be answered SOLELY on the basis of the information contained in the following passage.

Duplicating is the process of making a number of identical copies of letters, documents, etc. from an original. Some duplicating processes make copies directly from the original document. Other duplicating processes require the preparation of a special master, and copies are then made from the master. Four of the most common duplicating processes are stencil, fluid, offset, and xerox.

In the stencil process, the typewriter is used to cut the words into a master called a stencil. Drawings, charts, or graphs can be cut into the stencil using a stylus. As many as 3,500 good-quality copies can be reproduced from one stencil. Various grades of finished paper from inexpensive mimeograph to expensive bond can be used.

The fluid process is a good method of copying from 50 to 125 good-quality copies from a master, which is prepared with a special dye. The master is placed on the duplicator, and special paper with a hard finish is moistened and then passed through the duplicator. Some of the dye on the master is dissolved, creating an impression on the paper. The impression becomes lighter as more copies are made; and once the dye on the master is used up, a new master must be made.

The offset process is the most adaptable office duplicating process because this process can be used for making a few copies or many copies. Masters can be made on paper or plastic for a few hundred copies, or on metal plates for as many as 75,000 copies. By using a special technique called photo-offset, charts, photographs, illustrations, or graphs can be reproduced on the master plate. The offset process is capable of producing large quantities of fine, top-quality copies on all types of finished paper.

The xerox process reproduces an exact duplicate from an original. It is the fastest duplicating method because the original material is placed directly on the duplicator, eliminating the need to make a special master. Any kind of paper can be used. The xerox process is the most expensive duplicating process; however, it is the best method of reproducing small quantities of good-quality copies of reports, letters, official documents, memos, or contracts.

1. Of the following, the MOST efficient method of reproducing 5,000 copies of a graph is   1.____

    A. stencil   B. fluid   C. offset   D. xerox

2. The offset process is the MOST adaptable office duplicating process because   2.____

    A. it is the quickest duplicating method
    B. it is the least expensive duplicating method
    C. it can produce a small number or large number of copies
    D. a softer master can be used over and over again

3. Which one of the following duplicating processes uses moistened paper?   3.____

    A. Stencil   B. Fluid   C. Offset   D. Xerox

4. The fluid process would be the BEST process to use for reproducing   4.____

    A. five copies of a school transcript
    B. fifty copies of a memo
    C. five hundred copies of a form letter
    D. five thousand copies of a chart

5. Which one of the following duplicating processes does NOT require a special master?   5.____

    A. Fluid   B. Xerox   C. Offset   D. Stencil

6. Xerox is NOT used for all duplicating jobs because   6.____

    A. it produces poor-quality copies
    B. the process is too expensive
    C. preparing the master is too time-consuming
    D. it cannot produce written reports

7. Assume a city agency has 775 office workers.   7.____
If 2 out of 25 office workers were absent on a particular day, how many office workers reported to work on that day?

    A. 713   B. 744   C. 750   D. 773

Questions 8-11.

DIRECTIONS: In Questions 8 through 11, select the choice that is CLOSEST in meaning to the underlined word.

SAMPLE: This division reviews the <u>fiscal</u> reports of the agency.
In this sentence, the word <u>fiscal</u> means MOST NEARLY
    A. financial   B. critical   C. basic   D. personnel

    The correct answer is A, financial, because financial is closest to <u>fiscal</u>.

8. A central file eliminates the need to <u>retain</u> duplicate material.   8.____
The word <u>retain</u> means MOST NEARLY

    A. keep   B. change   C. locate   D. process

9. Filing is a <u>routine</u> office task.   9.____
<u>Routine</u> means MOST NEARLY

    A. proper   B. regular   C. simple   D. difficult

10. Sometimes a word, phrase, or sentence must be <u>deleted</u> to correct an error.   10.____
<u>Deleted</u> means MOST NEARLY

    A. removed   B. added   C. expanded   D. improved

11. Your supervisor will <u>evaluate</u> your work.
<u>Evaluate</u> means MOST NEARLY

    A. judge   B. list   C. assign   D. explain

11._____

Questions 12-19.

DIRECTIONS: The code table below shows 10 letters with matching numbers. For each Question 12 through 19, there are three sets of letters. Each set of letters is followed by a set of numbers which may or may not match their correct letter according to the code table. For each question, check all three sets of letters and numbers and mark your answer:
    A. if no pairs are correctly matched
    B. if only one pair is correctly matched
    C. if only two pairs are correctly matched
    D. if all three pairs are correctly matched

CODE TABLE

T	M	V	D	S	P	R	G	B	H
1	2	3	4	5	6	7	8	9	0

Sample Question: TMVDSP - 123456
                          RGBHTM - 789011
                          DSPRGB - 256789

In the sample question above, the first set of numbers correctly matches its set of letters. But the second and third pairs contain mistakes. In the second pair, M is incorrectly matched with number 1. According to the code table, letter M should be correctly matched with number 2. In the third pair, the letter D is incorrectly matched with number 2. According to the code table, letter D should be correctly matched with number 4. Since only one of the pairs is correctly matched, the answer to this sample question is B.

12.   RSBMRM -   759262
      GDSRVH -   845730
      VDBRTM -   349713

12._____

13.   TGVSDR -   183247
      SMHRDP -   520647
      TRMHSR -   172057

13._____

14.   DSPRGM -   456782
      MVDBHT -   234902
      HPMDBT -   062491

14._____

15.   BVPTRD -   936184
      GDPHMB -   807029
      GMRHMV -   827032

15._____

16.   MGVRSH -   283750
      TRDMBS -   174295
      SPRMGV -   567283

16._____

17.	SGBSDM	-	489542	17._____
	MGHPTM	-	290612	
	MPBMHT	-	269301	

18.	TDPBHM	-	146902	18._____
	VPBMRS	-	369275	
	GDMBHM	-	842902	

19.	MVPTBV	-	236194	19._____
	PDRTMB	-	647128	
	BGTMSM	-	981232	

Questions 20-25.

DIRECTIONS: In each of Questions 20 through 25, the names of four people are given. For each question, choose as your answer the one of the four names given which should be filed FIRST according to the usual system of alphabetical filing of names, as described in the following paragraph.

In filing names, you must start with the last name. Names are filed in order of the first letter of the last name, then the second letter, etc. Therefore, BAILY would be filed before BROWN, which would be filed before COLT. A name with fewer letters of the same type comes first; i.e., Smith before Smithe. If the last names are the same, the names are filed alphabetically by the first name. If the first name is an initial, a name with an initial would come before a first name that starts with the same letter as the initial. Therefore, I. BROWN would come before IRA BROWN. Finally, if both last name and first name are the same, the name would be filed alphabetically by the middle name, one again an initial coming before a middle name which starts with the same letter as the initial. If there is no middle name at all, the name would come before those with middle initials or names.

Sample Question: A.   Lester Daniels
                   B.   William Dancer
                   C.   Nathan Danzig
                   D.   Dan Lester

The last names beginning with D are filed before the last name beginning with L. Since DANIELS, DANCER, and DANZIG all begin with the same three letters, you must look at the fourth letter of the last name to determine which name should be filed first. C comes before I or Z in the alphabet, so DANCER is filed before DANIELS or DANZIG. Therefore, the answer to the above sample question is B.

| 20. | A. Scott Biala | B. Mary Byala | 20._____ |
| | C. Martin Baylor | D. Francis Bauer | |

| 21. | A. Howard J. Black | B. Howard Black | 21._____ |
| | C. J. Howard Black | D. John H. Black | |

| 22. | A. Theodora Garth Kingston | B. Theadore Barth Kingston | 22._____ |
| | C. Thomas Kingston | D. Thomas T. Kingston | |

| 23. | A. Paulette Mary Huerta | B. Paul M. Huerta | 23._____ |
| | C. Paulette L. Huerta | D. Peter A. Huerta | |

24.   A.   Martha Hunt Morgan   B.   Martin Hunt Morgan   24._____
       C.   Mary H. Morgan   D.   Martine H. Morgan

25.   A.   James T. Meerschaum   B.   James M. Mershum   25._____
       C.   James F. Mearshaum   D.   James N. Meshum

KEY (CORRECT ANSWERS)

1.	C		11.	A
2.	C		12.	B
3.	B		13.	B
4.	B		14.	C
5.	B		15.	A
6.	B		16.	D
7.	A		17.	A
8.	A		18.	D
9.	B		19.	A
10.	A		20.	D

21.	B
22.	B
23.	B
24.	A
25.	C

TEST 3

DIRECTIONS: Each question or incomplete statement is followed by several suggested answers or completions. Select the one that BEST answers the question or completes the statement. *PRINT THE LETTER OF THE CORRECT ANSWER IN THE SPACE AT THE RIGHT.*

1. Which one of the following statements about proper telephone usage is NOT always correct?
    When answering the telephone, you should

    A. know whom you are speaking to
    B. give the caller your undivided attention
    C. identify yourself to the caller
    D. obtain the information the caller wishes before you do your other work

1.____

2. Assume that, as a member of a worker's safety committee in your agency, you are responsible for encouraging other employees to follow correct safety practices. While you are working on your regular assignment, you observe an employee violating a safety rule.
    Of the following, the BEST action for you to take FIRST is to

    A. speak to the employee about safety practices and order him to stop violating the safety rule
    B. speak to the employee about safety practices and point out the safety rule he is violating
    C. bring the matter up in the next committee meeting
    D. report this violation of the safety rule to the employee's supervisor

2.____

3. Assume that you have been temporarily assigned by your supervisor to do a job which you do not want to do. The BEST action for you to take is to

    A. discuss the job with your supervisor, explaining why you do not want to do it
    B. discuss the job with your supervisor and tell her that you will not do it
    C. ask a co-worker to take your place on this job
    D. do some other job that you like; your supervisor may give the job you do not like to someone else

3.____

4. Assume that you keep the confidential personnel files of employees in your unit. A friend asks you to obtain some information from the file of one of your co-workers.
    The BEST action to take is to _____ to your friend.

    A. ask the co-worker if you can give the information
    B. ask your supervisor if you can give the information
    C. give the information
    D. refuse to give the information

4.____

Questions 5-8.

DIRECTIONS: Questions 5 through 8 are to be answered SOLELY on the basis of the information contained in the following passage.

City government is committed to providing a safe and healthy work environment for all city employees. An effective agency safety program reduces accidents by educating employees about the types of careless acts which can cause accidents. Even in an office, accidents can happen. If each employee is aware of possible safety hazards, the number of accidents on the job can be reduced.

Careless use of office equipment can cause accidents and injuries. For example, file cabinet drawers which are filled with papers can be so heavy that the entire cabinet could tip over from the weight of one open drawer.

The bottom drawers of desks and file cabinets should never be left open since employees could easily trip over open drawers and injure themselves.

When reaching for objects on a high shelf, an employee should use a strong, sturdy object such as a step stool to stand on. Makeshift platforms made out of books, papers, or boxes can easily collapse. Even chairs can slide out from under foot, causing serious injury.

Even at an employee's desk, safety hazards can occur. Frayed or cut wires should be repaired or replaced immediately. Computers which are not firmly anchored to the desk or table could fall, causing injury.

Smoking is one of the major causes of fires in the office. A lighted match or improperly extinguished cigarette thrown into a wastebasket filled with paper could cause a major fire with possible loss of life. Where smoking is permitted, ashtrays should be used. Smoking is particularly dangerous in offices where flammable chemicals are used.

5. The goal of an effective safety program is to   5._____

    A.   reduce office accidents
    B.   stop employees from smoking on the job
    C.   encourage employees to continue their education
    D.   eliminate high shelves in offices

6. Desks and file cabinets can become safety hazards when   6._____

    A.   their drawers are left open
    B.   they are used as wastebaskets
    C.   they are makeshift
    D.   they are not anchored securely to the floor

7. Smoking is especially hazardous when it occurs   7._____

    A.   near exposed wires
    B.   in a crowded office
    C.   in an area where flammable chemicals are used
    D.   where books and papers are stored

8. Accidents are likely to occur when   8._____

    A.   employees' desks are cluttered with books and papers
    B.   employees are not aware of safety hazards
    C.   employees close desk drawers
    D.   step stools are used to reach high objects

9. Assume that part of your job as a worker in the accounting division of a city agency is to   9.____
    answer the telephone. When you first answer the telephone, it is LEAST important to tell
    the caller

    A. your title   B. your name
    C. the name of your unit   D. the name of your agency

10. Assume that you are assigned to work as a receptionist, and your duties are to answer   10.____
    phones, greet visitors, and do other general office work. You are busy with a routine job
    when several visitors approach your desk.
    The BEST action to take is to

    A. ask the visitors to have a seat and assist them after your work is completed
    B. tell the visitors that you are busy and they should return at a more convenient time
    C. stop working long enough to assist the visitors
    D. continue working and wait for the visitors to ask you for assistance

11. Assume that your supervisor has chosen you to take a special course during working   11.____
    hours to learn a new payroll procedure. Although you know that you were chosen
    because of your good work record, a co-worker, who feels that he should have been cho-
    sen, has been telling everyone in your unit that the choice was unfair.
    Of the following, the BEST way to handle this situation FIRST is to   .

    A. suggest to the co-worker that everything in life is unfair
    B. contact your union representative in case your co-worker presents a formal griev-
        ance
    C. tell your supervisor about your co-worker's complaints and let her handle the situa-
        tion
    D. tell the co-worker that you were chosen because of your superior work record

12. Assume that while you are working on an assignment which must be completed quickly,   12.____
    a supervisor from another unit asks you to obtain information for her.
    Of the following, the BEST way to respond to her request is to

    A. tell her to return in an hour since you are busy
    B. give her the names of some people in her own unit who could help her
    C. tell her you are busy and refer her to a co-worker
    D. tell her that you are busy and ask her if she could wait until you finish your assign-
        ment

13. A co-worker in your unit is often off from work because of illness. Your supervisor assigns   13.____
    the co-worker's work to you when she is not there. Lately, doing her work has interfered
    with your own job.
    The BEST action for you to take FIRST is to

    A. discuss the problem with your supervisor
    B. complete your own work before starting your co-worker's work
    C. ask other workers in your unit to assist you
    D. work late in order to get the jobs done

14. During the month of June, 40,587 people attended a city-owned swimming pool. In July, 13,014 more people attended the swimming pool than the number that had attended in June. In August, 39,655 people attended the swimming pool.
    The TOTAL number of people who attended the swimming pool during the months of June, July, and August was

    A. 80,242   B. 93,256   C. 133,843   D. 210,382

14.____

Questions 15-22.

DIRECTIONS: Questions 15 through 22 test how well you understand what you read. It will be necessary for you to read carefully because your answers to these questions must be based ONLY on the information in the following paragraphs.

The telephone directory is made up of two books. The first book consists of the introductory section and the alphabetical listing of names section. The second book is the classified directory (also known as the yellow pages). Many people who are familiar with one book do not realize how useful the other can be. The efficient office worker should become familiar with both books in order to make the best use of this important source of information.

The introductory section gives general instructions for finding numbers in the alphabetical listing and classified directory. This section also explains how to use the telephone company's many services, including the operator and information services, gives examples of charges for local and long-distance calls, and lists area codes for the entire country. In addition, this section provides a useful postal zip code map.

The alphabetical listing of names section lists the names, addresses, and telephone numbers of subscribers in an area. Guide names, or *telltales,* are on the top corner of each page. These guide names indicate the first and last name to be found on that page. *Telltales* help locate any particular name quickly. A cross-reference spelling is also given to help locate names which are spelled several different ways. City, state, and federal government agencies are listed under the major government heading. For example, an agency of the federal government would be listed under *United States Government.*

The classified directory, or yellow pages, is a separate book. In this section are advertising services, public transportation line maps, shopping guides, and listings of businesses arranged by the type of product or services they offer. This book is most useful when looking for the name or phone number of a business when all that is known is the type of product offered and the address, or when trying to locate a particular type of business in an area. Businesses listed in the classified directory can usually be found in the alphabetical listing of names section. When the name of the business is known, you will find the address or phone number more quickly in the alphabetical listing of names section.

15. The introductory section provides

    A. shopping guides   B. government listings
    C. business listings   D. information services

15.____

16. Advertising services would be found in the

    A. introductory section   B. alphabetical listing of names section
    C. classified directory   D. information services

16.____

17. According to the information in the above passage for locating government agencies, the
Information Office of the Department of Consumer Affairs of New York City government
would be alphabetically listed FIRST under

    A. *I* for Information Offices
    B. *D* for Department of Consumer Affairs
    C. *N* for New York City
    D. *G* for government

17._____

18. When the name of a business is known, the QUICKEST way to find the phone number is
to look in the

    A. classified directory
    B. introductory section
    C. alphabetical listing of names section
    D. advertising service section

18.__ _

19. The QUICKEST way to find the phone number of a business when the type of service a
business offers and its address is known is to look in the

    A. classified directory
    B. alphabetical listing of names section
    C. introductory section
    D. information service

19._____

20. What is a *telltale?*

    A. An alphabetical listing
    B. A guide name
    C. A map
    D. A cross-reference listing

20._____

21. The BEST way to find a postal zip code is to look in the

    A. classified directory
    B. introductory section
    C. alphabetical listing of names section
    D. government heading

21._____

22. To help find names which have several different spellings, the telephone directory provides

    A. cross-reference spelling   B. *telltales*
    C. spelling guides   D. advertising services

22._____

23. Assume that your agency has been given $2025 to purchase file cabinets.
If each file cabinet costs $135, how many file cabinets can your agency purchase?

    A. 8   B. 10   C. 15   D. 16

23._____

24. Assume that your unit ordered 14 staplers at a total cost of $30.20, and each stapler cost   24.____
the same.
The cost of one stapler was MOST NEARLY

    A. $1.02   B. $1.61   C. $2.16   D. $2.26

25. Assume that you are responsible for counting and recording licensing fees collected by   25.____
your department. On a particular day, your department collected in fees 40 checks in the
amount of $6 each, 80 checks in the amount of $4 each, 45 twenty dollar bills, 30 ten dollar bills, 42 five dollar bills, and 186 one dollar bills.
The TOTAL amount in fees collected on that day was

    A. $1,406   B. $1,706   C. $2,156   D. $2,356

26. Assume that you are responsible for your agency's petty cash fund. During the month of   26.____
February, you pay out 7 $2.00 subway fares and one taxi fare for $10.85. You pay out
nothing else from the fund. At the end of February, you count the money left in the fund
and find 3 one dollar bills, 4 quarters, 5 dimes, and 4 nickels. The amount of money you
had available in the petty cash fund at the BEGINNING of February was

    A. $4.70   B. $16.35   C. $24.85   D. $29.55

27. You overhear your supervisor criticize a co-worker for handling equipment in an unsafe   27.____
way. You feel that the criticism may be unfair.
Of the following, it would be BEST for you to

    A. take your co-worker aside and tell her how you feel about your supervisor's com-
ments
    B. interrupt the discussion and defend your co-worker to your supervisor
    C. continue working as if you had not overheard the discussion
    D. make a list of other workers who have violated safety rules and give it to your
supervisor

28. Assume that you have been assigned to work on a long-term project with an employee   28.____
who is known for being uncooperative.
In beginning to work with this employee, it would be LEAST desirable for you to

    A. understand why the person is uncooperative
    B. act in a calm manner rather than an emotional manner
    C. be appreciative of the co-worker's work
    D. report the co-worker's lack of cooperation to your supervisor

29. Assume that you are assigned to sell tickets at a city-owned ice skating rink. An adult   29.____
ticket costs $4.50, and a children's ticket costs $2.25. At the end of a day, you find that
you have sold 36 adult tickets and 80 children's tickets.
The TOTAL amount of money you collected for that day was

    A. $244.80   B. $318.00   C. $342.00   D. $348.00

30. If each office worker files 487 index cards in one hour, how many cards can 26 office   30.____
workers file in one hour?

    A. 10,662   B. 12,175   C. 12,662   D. 14,266

KEY (CORRECT ANSWERS)

1.	D	16.	C
2.	B	17.	C
3.	A	18.	C
4.	D	19.	A
5.	A	20.	B
6.	A	21.	B
7.	C	22.	A
8.	B	23.	C
9.	A	24.	C
10.	C	25.	C
11.	C	26.	D
12.	D	27.	C
13.	A	28.	D
14.	C	29.	C
15.	D	30.	C

EXAMINATION SECTION
TEST 1

DIRECTIONS: Each question or incomplete statement is followed by several suggested answers or completions. Select the one that BEST answers the question or completes the statement. *PRINT THE LETTER OF THE CORRECT ANSWER IN THE SPACE AT THE RIGHT.*

1. If you open a personal letter by mistake, the one of the following actions which it would generally be BEST for you to take is to   1.____

    A. ignore your error, attach the envelope to the letter, and distribute in the usual manner
    B. personally give the addressee the letter without any explanation
    C. place the letter inside the envelope, indicate under your initials that it was opened in error, and give to the addressee
    D. reseal the envelope or place the contents in another envelope and pass on to addressee

2. If you receive a telephone call regarding a matter which your office does not handle, you should FIRST   2.____

    A. give the caller the telephone number of the proper office so that he can dial again
    B. offer to transfer the caller to the proper office
    C. suggest that the caller re-dial since he probably dialed incorrectly
    D. tell the caller he has reached the wrong office and then hang up

3. When you answer the telephone, the MOST important reason for identifying yourself and your organization is to   3.____

    A. give the caller time to collect his or her thoughts
    B. impress the caller with your courtesy
    C. inform the caller that he or she has reached the right number
    D. set a business-like tone at the beginning of the conversation

4. The one of the following cases in which you would NOT place a special notation in the left margin of a letter that you have typed is when   4.____

    A. one of the copies is intended for someone other than the addressee of the letter
    B. you enclose a flyer with the letter
    C. you sign your superior's name to the letter, at his or her request
    D. the letter refers to something being sent under separate cover

5. Suppose that you accidentally cut a letter or enclosure as you are opening an envelope with a paper knife.
The one of the following that you should do FIRST is to   5.____

    A. determine whether the document is important
    B. clip or staple the pieces together and process as usual
    C. mend the cut document with transparent tape
    D. notify the sender that the communication was damaged and request another copy

6. As soon as you pick up the phone, a very angry caller begins immediately to complain   6._____
about city agencies and *red tape*. He says that he has been shifted to two or three different offices. It turns out that he is seeking information which is not immediately available
to you. You believe you know, however, where it can be found.
Which of the following actions is the BEST one for you to take?

   A. To eliminate all confusion, suggest that the caller write the mayor stating explicitly
      what he wants.
   B. Apologize by telling the caller how busy city agencies now are, but also tell him
      directly that you do not have the information he needs.
   C. Ask for the caller's telephone number, and assure him you will call back after you
      have checked further.
   D. Give the caller the name and telephone number of the person who might be able to
      help, but explain that you are not positive he will get results.

7. Suppose that one of your duties is to dictate responses to routine requests from the pub-   7._____
lic for information. A letter writer asks for information which, as expressed in a one-sen-
tence, explicit agency rule, cannot be given out to the public.
Of the following ways of answering the letter, which is the MOST efficient?

   A. Quote verbatim that section of the agency rules which prohibits giving this informa-
      tion to the public.
   B. Without quoting the rule, explain why you cannot accede to the request and sug-
      gest alternative sources.
   C. Describe how carefully the request was considered before classifying it as subject
      to the rule forbidding the issuance of such information.
   D. Acknowledge receipt of the letter and advise that the requested information is not
      released to the public.

8. Suppose you assist in supervising a staff which has rather high morale, and your own   8._____
supervisor asks you to poll the staff to find out who will be able to work overtime this particular evening to help complete emergency work.
Which of the following approaches would be MOST likely to win their cooperation while
maintaining their morale?

   A. Tell them that the better assignments will be given only to those who work over-
      time.
   B. Tell them that occasional overtime is a job requirement.
   C. Assure them they'll be doing you a personal favor.
   D. Let them know clearly why the overtime is needed.

9. Suppose that you have been asked to write and to prepare for reproduction new depart-   9._____
mental vacation leave regulations.
After you have written the new regulations, all of which fit on two pages, which one of
the following would be the BEST method of reproducing 1,000 copies?

   A. An outside private printer because you can best maintain confidentiality using this
      technique
   B. Photocopying because the copies will have the best possible appearance
   C. Sending the file to all department employees as printable PDFs
   D. Printing and collating on the office high-volume printer

10. You are in charge of verifying employees' qualifications. This involves telephoning previ-   10.____
ous employers and schools. One of the applications which you are reviewing contains
information which you are almost certain is correct on the basis of what the employee
has told you.
The BEST thing to do is to

    A. check the information again with the employer
    B. perform the required verification procedures
    C. accept the information as valid
    D. ask a superior to verify the information

11. The practice of immediately identifying oneself and one's place of employment when   11.____
contacting persons on the telephone is

    A. *good* because the receiver of the call can quickly identify the caller and establish a
frame of reference
    B. *good* because it helps to set the caller at ease with the other party
    C. *poor* because it is not necessary to divulge that information when making general
calls
    D. *poor* because it takes longer to arrive at the topic to be discussed

12. Which one of the following should be the MOST important overall consideration when   12.____
preparing a recommendation to automate a large-scale office activity?
The

    A. number of models of automated equipment available
    B. benefits and costs of automation
    C. fears and resistance of affected employees
    D. experience of offices which have automated similar activities

13. A tickler file is MOST appropriate for filing materials   13.____

    A. chronologically according to date they were received
    B. alphabetically by name
    C. alphabetically by subject
    D. chronologically according to date they should be followed up

14. Which of the following is the BEST reason for decentralizing rather then centralizing the   14.____
use of duplicating machines?

    A. Developing and retaining efficient duplicating machine operators
    B. Facilitating supervision of duplicating services
    C. Motivating employees to produce legible duplicated copies
    D. Placing the duplicating machines where they are most convenient and most fre-
quently used

15. Window envelopes are sometimes considered preferable to individually addressed enve-   15.____
lopes PRIMARILY because

    A. window envelopes are available in standard sizes for all purposes
    B. window envelopes are more attractive and official-looking
    C. the use of window envelopes eliminates the risk of inserting a letter in the wrong
envelope
    D. the use of window envelopes requires neater typing

16. In planning the layout of a new office, the utilization of space and the arrangement of staff, furnishings, and equipment should usually be MOST influenced by the

    A. gross square footage
    B. status differences in the chain of command
    C. framework of informal relationships among employees
    D. activities to be performed

16._____

17. Office forms sometimes consist of several copies, each of a different color. The MAIN reason for using different colors is to

    A. make a favorable impression on the users of the form
    B. distinguish each copy from the others
    C. facilitate the preparation of legible carbon copies
    D. reduce cost, since using colored stock permits recycling of paper

17._____

18. Which of the following is the BEST justification for obtaining a photocopying machine for the office?

    A. A photocopying machine can produce an unlimited number of copies at a low fixed cost per copy.
    B. Employees need little training in operating a photocopying machine.
    C. Office costs will be reduced and efficiency increased.
    D. The legibility of a photocopy generally is superior to copy produced by any other office duplicating device.

18._____

19. An administrative officer in charge of a small fund for buying office supplies has just written a check to Charles Laird, a supplier, and has sent the check by messenger to him. A half-hour later, the messenger telephones the administrative officer. He has lost the check.
Which of the following is the MOST important action for the administrative officer to take under these circumstances?

    A. Ask the messenger to return and write a report describing the loss of the check.
    B. Make a note on the performance record of the messenger who lost the check.
    C. Take the necessary steps to have payment stopped on the check.
    D. Refrain from doing anything since the check may be found shortly.

19._____

20. A petty cash fund is set up PRIMARILY to

    A. take care of small investments that must be made from time to time
    B. take care of small expenses that arise from time to time
    C. provide a fund to be used as the office wants to use it with little need to maintain records
    D. take care of expenses that develop during emergencies such as machine breakdowns and fires

20._____

21. Your superior has asked you to send a package from your agency to a government agency in another city. He has written out the message and has indicated the name of the government agency.
When you prepare the package for mailing, which of the following items that your superior has not mentioned must you be sure to include?

21._____

A. Today's date
B. The full address of the government agency
C. A polite opening such as *Dear Sirs*
D. A final sentence such as *We would appreciate hearing from your agency in reply as soon as is convenient for you*

22. In addition to the original piece of correspondence, one should USUALLY also have typed

    22.____

    A. a single copy
    B. as many copies as can be typed at one time
    C. no more copies than are needed
    D. two copies

23. The one of the following which is the BEST procedure to follow when making a short insert in a completed dictation is to

    23.____

    A. label the insert with a letter and indicate the position of the insert in the text by writing the identifying letter in the proper place
    B. squeeze the insert into its proper place within the main text of the dictation
    C. take down the insert and check the placement with the person who dictated when you are ready to transcribe your notes
    D. transcribe the dictation into longhand, including the insert in its proper position

24. The one of the following procedures which will be MOST efficient in helping you to quickly open your dictation notebook to a clean sheet is to

    24.____

    A. clip or place a rubberband around the used portion of the notebook
    B. leave the book out and open to a clean page when not in use
    C. transcribe each dictation after it is given and rip out the used pages
    D. use a book marker to indicate which portion of the notebook has been used

25. The purpose of dating your dictation notebooks is GENERALLY to

    25.____

    A. enable you to easily refer to your notes at a later date
    B. ensure that you transcribe your notes in the order in which they were dictated
    C. set up a precise record-keeping procedure
    D. show your employer that you pay attention to detail

———

KEY (CORRECT ANSWERS)

1.	C		11.	A
2.	B		12.	B
3.	C		13.	D
4.	C		14.	D
5.	C		15.	C
6.	C		16.	D
7.	A		17.	B
8.	D		18.	C
9.	D		19.	C
10.	B		20.	B

21.	B
22.	C
23.	A
24.	A
25.	A

———

TEST 2

DIRECTIONS: Each question or incomplete statement is followed by several suggested answers or completions. Select the one that BEST answers the question or completes the statement. *PRINT THE LETTER OF THE CORRECT ANSWER IN THE SPACE AT THE RIGHT.*

1. With regard to typed correspondence received by most offices, which of the following is the GREATEST problem?

    A. Verbosity   B. Illegibility
    C. Improper folding   D. Excessive copies

1.____

2. Of the following, the GREATEST advantage of flash drives over rewritable CD storage is that they

    A. are portable
    B. are both smaller and lighter
    C. contain more storage space
    D. allow files to be deleted to free space

2.____

3. Suppose that a large quantity of information is in the files which are located a good distance from your desk. Almost every worker in your office must use these files constantly. Your duties in particular require that you daily refer to about 25 of the same items. They are short, one-page items distributed throughout the files. In this situation, your BEST course would be to

    A. take the items that you use daily from the files and keep them on your desk, inserting *out cards* in their place
    B. go to the files each time you need the information so that the items will be there when other workers need them
    C. make xerox copies of the information you use most frequently and keep them in your desk for ready reference
    D. label the items you use most often with different colored tabs for immediate identification

3.____

4. Of the following, the MOST important advantage of preparing manuals of office procedures in loose-leaf form is that this form

    A. permits several employees to use different sections simultaneously
    B. facilitates the addition of new material and the removal of obsolete material
    C. is more readily arranged in alphabetical order
    D. reduces the need for cross-references to locate material carried under several headings

4.____

5. Suppose that you establish a new clerical procedure for the unit you supervise. Your keeping a close check on the time required by your staff to handle the new procedure is WISE mainly because such a check will find out

    A. whether your subordinates know how to handle the new procedure
    B. whether a revision of the unit's work schedule will be necessary as a result of the new procedure
    C. what attitude your employees have toward the new procedure
    D. what alterations in job descriptions will be necessitated by the new procedure

5.____

6. The numbered statements below relate to the stenographic skill of taking dictation. According to authorities on secretarial practices, which of these are generally recommended guides to development of efficient stenographic skills?　　　　6.____

STATEMENTS

1. A stenographer should date her notebook daily to facilitate locating certain notes at a later time.
2. A stenographer should make corrections of grammatical mistakes while her boss is dictating to her.
3. A stenographer should draw a line through the dictated matter in her notebook after she has transcribed it.
4. A stenographer should write in longhand unfamiliar names and addresses dictated to her.

The CORRECT answer is:

   A. Only Statements 1, 2, and 3 are generally recommended guides.
   B. Only Statements 2, 3, and 4 are generally recommended guides.
   C. Only Statements 1, 3, and 4 are generally recommended guides.
   D. All four statements are generally recommended guides.

7. According to generally recognized rules of filing in an alphabetic filing system, the one of the following names which normally should be filed LAST is　　　　7.____

   A. Department of Education, New York State
   B. F.B.I.
   C. Police Department of New York City
   D. P.S. 81 of New York City

8. Which one of the following forms for the typed name of the dictator in the closing lines of a letter is generally MOST acceptable in the United States?　　　　8.____

   A. (Dr.) James F. Fenton
   B. Dr. James F. Fenton
   C. Mr. James F. Fenton, Ph.D.
   D. James F. Fenton

9. Which of the following is, MOST generally, a rule to be followed when typing a rough draft?　　　　9.____

   A. The copy should be single spaced.
   B. The copy should be triple spaced.
   C. There is no need for including footnotes.
   D. Errors must be neatly corrected.

10. An office assistant needs a synonym.
Of the following, the book which she would find MOST useful is　　　　10.____

   A. a world atlas
   B. BARTLETT'S FAMILIAR QUOTATIONS
   C. a manual of style
   D. a thesaurus

11. Of the following examples of footnotes, the one that is expressed in the MOST generally   11.____
accepted standard form is:

   A. Johnson, T.F. (Dr.), <u>English for Everyone</u>, 3rd or 4th edition; New York City Linton
       Publishing Company, p. 467
   B. Frank Taylor, <u>English for Today</u> (New York: Rayton Publishing Company, 1971), p.
       156
   C. Ralph Wilden, <u>English for Tomorrow,</u> Reynolds Publishing Company, England, p.
       451
   D. Quinn, David, Yesterday's English (New York: Baldwin Publishing Company, 1972),
       p. 431

12. Standard procedures are used in offices PRIMARILY because   12.____

   A. an office is a happier place if everyone is doing the tasks in the same manner
   B. particular ways of doing jobs are considered more efficient than other ways
   C. it is good discipline for workers to follow standard procedures approved by the
       supervisor
   D. supervisors generally don't want workers to be creative in planning their work

13. Assume that an office assistant has the responsibility for compiling, typing, and mailing a   13.____
preliminary announcement of Spring term course offerings. The announcement will go
to approximately 900 currently enrolled students. Assuming that the following equipment
is available for use, the MOST EFFECTIVE method for distributing the announcement
to all 900 students is to

   A. e-mail it as a text document using the electronic student mailing list
   B. post the announcement as a PDF document for download on the department website
   C. send it by fax
   D. post the announcement and leave copies in buildings around campus

14. *Justified typing* is a term that refers MOST specifically to typewriting copy   14.____

   A. that has been edited and for which final copy is being prepared
   B. in a form that allows for an even right-hand margin
   C. with a predetermined vertical placement for each alternate line
   D. that has been approved by the supervisor and his superior

15. Which one of the following is the BEST form for the address in a letter?   15.____

   A. Mr. John Jones
       Vice President, The Universal Printing Company
       1220 Fifth Avenue
       New York, 10023 New York
   B. Mr. John Jones, Vice President
       The Universal Printing Company
       1220 Fifth Avenue
       New York, New York 10023
   C. Mr. John Jones, Vice President, The Universal Printing Company
       1220 Fifth Avenue
       New York, New York 10023

D. Mr. John Jones Vice President,
The Universal Printing Company
1220 Fifth Avenue
New York, 10023 New York

16. Of the following, the CHIEF advantage of the use of window envelopes over ordinary envelopes is that window envelopes

    A. eliminate the need for addressing envelopes
    B. protect the confidential nature of enclosed material
    C. cost less to buy than ordinary envelopes
    D. reduce the danger of the address becoming illegible

16.____

17. In the complimentary close of a business letter, the FIRST letter of _____ should be capitalized.

    A. all the words   B. none of the words
    C. only the first word   D. only the last word

17.____

18. Assume that one of your duties is to procure needed office supplies from the supply room. You are permitted to draw supplies every two weeks.
The one of the following which would be the MOST desirable practice for you to follow in obtaining supplies is to

    A. obtain a quantity of supplies sufficient to last for several months to make certain that enough supplies are always on hand
    B. determine the minimum supply necessary to keep on hand for the various items and obtain an additional quantity as soon as possible after the supply on hand has been reduced to this minimum
    C. review the supplies once a month to determine what items have been exhausted and obtain an additional quantity as soon as possible
    D. obtain a supply of an item as soon after it has been exhausted as is possible

18.____

19. Some offices that keep carbon copies of letters use several different colors of carbon paper for making carbon copies.
Of the following, the CHIEF reason for using different colors of carbon paper is to

    A. facilitate identification of different types of letters in the files
    B. relieve the monotony of typing and filing carbon copies
    C. reduce the costs of preparing carbon copies
    D. utilize both sides of the carbon paper for typing

19.____

20. Your supervisor asks you to post an online ad for freelance designers interested in submitting samples for a new company logo. Prospective workers should be proficient in which of the following software?

    A. Microsoft Word   B. Adobe Acrobat Pro
    C. Adobe Illustrator   D. Microsoft PowerPoint

20.____

21. Gary Thompson is applying for a position with the firm of Gray and Williams.
Which letter should be filed in top position in the *Application* folder?

    A. A letter of recommendation written on September 18 by Johnson & Smith
    B. Williams' letter of October 8 requesting further details regarding Thompson's experience

21.____

C. Thompson's letter of September 8 making application for a position as sales manager
D. Letter of September 20 from Alfred Jackson recommending Thompson for the job

22. The USUAL arrangement in indexing the names of the First National Bank, Toledo, is   22.____

   A. First National Bank, Toledo, Ohio
   B. Ohio, First National Bank, Toledo
   C. Toledo, First National Bank, Ohio
   D. Ohio, Toledo, First National Bank

23. A single line through typed text indicating that it's incorrect or invalid is known as a(n)   23.____

   A. underline
   B. strikethrough
   C. line font
   D. eraser

24. A typical e-mail with an attachment should contain all of the following for successful transmittal EXCEPT   24.____

   A. recipient's address   B. file attachment
   C. body text   D. description of attachment

25. The subject line in a letter is USUALLY typed a _____ space below the _____.   25.____

   A. single; inside address   B. single; salutation
   C. double; inside address   D. double; salutation

KEY (CORRECT ANSWERS)

1.	A	11.	B
2.	C	12.	B
3.	C	13.	A
4.	B	14.	B
5.	B	15.	B
6.	C	16.	A
7.	D	17.	C
8.	D	18.	B
9.	B	19.	A
10.	D	20.	C

21.	B
22.	A
23.	B
24.	D
25.	D

EXAMINATION SECTION
TEST 1

DIRECTIONS: Each question or incomplete statement is followed by several suggested answers or completions. Select the one that BEST answers the question or completes the statement. *PRINT THE LETTER OF THE CORRECT ANSWER IN THE SPACE AT THE RIGHT.*

Questions 1-22.

DIRECTIONS: Read through each group of words. Indicate in the space at the right the letter of the misspelled word.

1. A. miniature   B. recession   1.____
     C. accommodate   D. supress

2. A. mortgage   B. illogical   2.____
     C. fasinate   D. pronounce

3. A. calendar   B. heros   3.____
     C. ecstasy   D. librarian

4. A. initiative   B. extraordinary   4.____
     C. villian   D. exaggerate

5. A. absence   B. sense   5.____
     C. dosn't   D. height

6. A. curiosity   B. ninety   6.____
     C. truely   D. grammar

7. A. amateur   B. definate   7.____
     C. meant   D. changeable

8. A. excellent   B. studioes   8.____
     C. achievement   D. weird

9. A. goverment   B. description   9.____
     C. sergeant   D. desirable

10. A. proceed   B. anxious   10.____
     C. neice   D. precede

11. A. environment   B. omitted   11.____
     C. apparant   D. misconstrue

12. A. comparative   B. hindrance   12.____
     C. benefited   D. unamimous

13. A. embarrass   B. recommend   13.____
     C. desciple   D. argument

14. A. sophomore   B. superintendent   14.____
     C. concievable   D. disastrous

15. A. agressive   B. questionnaire   15.___
     C. occurred   D. rhythm

16. A. peaceable   B. conscientious   16.___
     C. redicule   D. deterrent

17. A. mischievious   B. writing   17.___
     C. competition   D. athletics

18. A. auxiliary   B. synonymous   18.___
     C. maneuver   D. repitition

19. A. existence   B. optomistic   19.___
     C. acquitted   D. tragedy

20. A. hypocrisy   B. parrallel   20.___
     C. exhilaration   D. prevalent

21. A. convalesence   B. infallible   21.___
     C. destitute   D. grotesque

22. A. magnanimity   B. asassination   22.___
     C. incorrigible   D. pestilence

Questions 23-40.

DIRECTIONS: In Questions 23 through 40, one sentence fragment contains an error in
               punctuation or capitalization. Indicate the letter of the INCORRECT sentence
               fragment and place it in space at the right.

23. A. Despite a year's work   23.___
     B. in a well-equipped laboratory,
     C. my Uncle failed to complete his research;
     D. now he will never graduate.

24. A. Gene, if you are going to sleep   24.___
     B. all afternoon I will enter
     C. that ladies' golf tournament
     D. sponsored by the Chamber of Commerce.

25. A. Seeing the cat slink toward the barn,   25.___
     B. the farmer's wife jumped off the
     C. ladder picked up a broom, and began
     D. shouting at the top of her voice.

26. A. Extending over southeast Idaho and   26.___
     B. northwest Wyoming, the Tetons
     C. are noted for their height; however the
     D. highest peak is actually under 14,000 feet.

27.   A.   "Sarah, can you recall the name   27._____
      B.   of the English queen
      C.   who supposedly said, 'We are not
      D.   amused?'"

28.   A.   My aunt's graduation present to me   28._____
      B.   cost, I imagine more than she could
      C.   actually afford. It's a
      D.   Swiss watch with numerous features.

29.   A.   On the left are examples of buildings   29._____
      B.   from the Classical Period; two temples
      C.   one of which was dedicated to Zeus; the
      D.   Agora, a marketplace; and a large arch.

30.   A.   Tired of sonic booms, the people who   30._____
      B.   live near Springfield's Municipal Airport
      C.   formed an anti noise organization
      D.   with the amusing name of Sound Off.

31.   A.   "Joe, Mrs. Sweeney said, "your family   31._____
      B.   arrives Sunday. Since you'll be in
      C.   the Labor Day parade, we could ask Mr.
      D.   Krohn, who has a big car, to meet them."

32.   A.   The plumber emerged from the basement and   32._____
      B.   said, "Mr. Cohen I found the trouble in
      C.   your water heater. Could you move those
      D.   Schwinn bikes out of my way?"

33.   A.   The President walked slowly to the   33._____
      B.   podium, bowed to Edward Everett Hale
      C.   the other speaker, and began his formal address:
      D.   "Fourscore and seven years ago...."

34.   A.   Mr. Fontana, I hope, will arrive before   34._____
      B.   the beginning of the ceremonies; however,
      C.   if his plane is delayed, I have a substitute
      D.   speaker who can be here at a moments' notice.

35.   A.   Gladys wedding dress, a satin creation,   35._____
      B.   lay crumpled on the floor; her veil,
      C.   torn and streaked, lay nearby. "Jilted!"
      D.   shrieked Gladys. She was clearly annoyed.

36.   A.   Although it is poor grammar, the word   36._____
      B.   hopefully has become television's newest
      C.   pet expression; I hope (to use the correct
      D.   form) that it will soon pass from favor.

37. A.
     B.
     C.
     D.

                Plaza Apartment Hotel

                103 Tower road

                Hampstead, Iowa 52025

                March 13, 2008

37.___

38. A. Circulation Department
     B. British History Illustrated
     C. 3000 Walnut Street
     D. Boulder Colorado 80302

38.___

39. A. Dear Sirs:
     B.   Last spring I ordered a subscription to your
     C. magazine. I had read and enjoyed the May
     D. issue containing the article titled "kings."

39.___

40. A.   I have not however, received a
     B. single issue. Will you check this?
     C. Sincerely,
     D. Maria Herrera

40.___

Questions 41-70.

DIRECTIONS: Questions 41 through 70 represent common grammatical concerns: subject-verb agreement, appropriate use of pronouns, and appropriate use of verbs. Read each sentence and indicate the letter of the grammatically CORRECT answer in the space at the right.

41. THE REIVERS, one of William Faulkner's last works, _____ made into a movie starring Steve McQueen.

    A. has been   B. have been
    C. are being   D. were

41.___

42. He _____ on the ground, his eyes fastened on an ant slowly pushing a morsel of food toward the ant hill.

    A. layed   B. laid   C. had laid   D. lay

42.___

43. Nobody in the tri-cities _____ to admit that a flood could be disastrous.

    A. are willing   B. have been willing
    C. is willing   D. were willing

43.___

44. "_____," the senator asked, "have you convinced to run against the incumbent?"

    A. Who   B. Whom   C. Whomever   D. Whomsoever

44.___

45. Of all the psychology courses that I took, Statistics 101 _____ the most demanding.

    A. was   B. are   C. is   D. were

45.___

46. Neither the conductor nor the orchestra members _____ the music to be applauded so enthusiastically.   46._____

    A. were expecting   B. was expecting
    C. is expected   D. has been expecting

47. The requirements for admission to the Lettermen's Club _____ posted outside the athletic director's office for months.   47._____

    A. was   B. was being
    C. has been   D. have been

48. Please give me a list of the people _____ to compete in the kayak race.   48._____

    A. whom you think have planned
    B. who you think has planned
    C. who you think is planning
    D. who you think are planning

49. I saw Eloise and Abelard earlier today; _____ were riding around in a fancy 1956 MG.   49._____

    A. she and him   B. her and him
    C. she and he   D. her and he

50. If you _____ the trunk in the attic, I'll unpack it later today.   50._____

    A. can sit   B. are able to sit
    C. can set   D. have sat

51. _____ all of the flour been used, or may I borrow three cups?   51._____

    A. Have   B. Has   C. Is   D. Could

52. In exasperation, the cycle shop's owner suggested that _____ there too long.   52._____

    A. us boys were   B. we boys were
    C. us boys had been   D. we boys had been

53. Idleness as well as money _____ the root of all evil.   53._____

    A. have been   B. were to have been
    C. is   D. are

54. Only the string players from the quartet – Gregory, Isaac, _____ - remained after the concert to answer questions.   54._____

    A. him, and I   B. he, and I
    C. him, and me   D. he, and me

55. Of all the antiques that _____ for sale, Gertrude chose to buy a stupid glass thimble.   55._____

    A. was   B. is
    C. would have   D. were

56. The detective snapped, "Don't confuse me with theories about _____ you believe committed the crime!"   56._____

    A. who   B. whom   C. whomever   D. which

57. _____ when we first called, we might have avoided our present predicament.   57.____

    A. The plumber's coming
    B. If the plumber would have come
    C. If the plumber had come
    D. If the plumber was to have come

58. We thought the sun _____ in the north until we discovered that our compass was defec-   58.____
tive.

    A. had rose   B. had risen
    C. had rised   D. had raised

59. Each play of Shakespeare's _____ more than _____ share of memorable characters.   59.____

    A. contain; its   B. contains; its
    C. contains; it's   D. contain; their

60. Our English teacher suggested to _____ seniors that either Tolstoy or Dickens _____   60.____
the outstanding novelist of the nineteenth century.

    A. we; was considered   B. we; were considered
    C. us; was considered   D. us; were considered

61. Sherlock Holmes, together with his great friend and companion Dr. Watson, _____ to   61.____
aid the woman _____ had stumbled into the room.

    A. has agreed; who   B. have agreed; whom
    C. has agreed; whom   D. have agreed; who

62. Several of the deer _____ when they spotted my backpack _____ open in the   62.____
meadow.

    A. was frightened; laying   B. were frightened; lying
    C. were frightened; laying   D. was frightened; lying

63. After the Scholarship Committee announces _____ selection, hysterics often _____.   63.____

    A. it's; occur   B. its; occur
    C. their; occur   D. their; occurs

64. I _____ the key on the table last night so you and _____ could find it.   64.____

    A. layed; her   B. lay; she
    C. laid; she   D. laid; her

65. Some of the antelope _____ wandered away from the meadow where the rancher   65.____
_____ the block of salt.

    A. has; sat   B. has; set
    C. have; had set   D. has; sets

66. Macaroni and cheese _____ best to us (that is, to Andy and _____) when Mother adds   66.____
extra cheddar cheese.

    A. tastes; I   B. tastes; me
    C. taste; me   D. taste; I

67. Frank said, "It must have been _____ called the phone company."   67.____

    A. she who   B. she whom
    C. her who   D. her whom

68. The herd _____ moving restlessly at every bolt of lightning; it was either Ted or _____   68.____
    who saw the beginning of the stampede.

    A. was; me   B. were; I
    C. was; I   D. have been; me

69. The foreman _____ his lateness by saying that his alarm clock _____ until six minutes   69.____
    before eight.

    A. explains; had not rang
    B. explained; has not rung
    C. has explained; rung
    D. explained; hadn't rung

70. Of all the coaches, Ms. Cox is the only one who _____ that Sherry dives more grace-   70.____
    fully than _____.

    A. is always saying; I
    B. is always saying; me
    C. are always saying; I
    D. were always saying; me

Questions 71-90.

DIRECTIONS: Choose the word in Questions 71 through 90 that is MOST opposite in mean-
                     ing to the italicized word.

71. *fact*   71.____

    A. statistic   B. statement
    C. incredible   D. conjecture

72. *stiff*   72.____

    A. fastidious   B. babble
    C. supple   D. apprehensive

73. *blunt*   73.____

    A. concise   B. tactful
    C. artistic   D. humble

74. *foreign*   74.____

    A. pertinent   B. comely
    C. strange   D. scrupulous

75. *anger*   75.____

    A. infer   B. pacify   C. taint   D. revile

76. *frank*   76.____

    A. earnest   B. reticent   C. post   D. expensive

77. *secure*   77.____

    A. precarious   B. acquire   C. moderate   D. frenzied

78. *petty*   78.____

    A. harmonious   B. careful   C. forthright   D. momentous

79. *concede*   79.____

    A. dispute   B. reciprocate
    C. subvert   D. propagate

80. *benefit*   80.____

    A. liquidation   B. bazaar
    C. detriment   D. profit

81. *capricious*   81.____

    A. preposterous   B. constant
    C. diabolical   D. careless

82. *boisterous*   82.____

    A. devious   B. valiant   C. girlish   D. taciturn

83. *harmony*   83.____

    A. congruence   B. discord   C. chagrin   D. melody

84. *laudable*   84.____

    A. auspicious   B. despicable
    C. acclaimed   D. doubtful

85. *adherent*   85.____

    A. partisan   B. stoic   C. renegade   D. recluse

86. *exuberant*   86.____

    A. frail   B. corpulent   C. austere   D. bigot

87. *spurn*   87.____

    A. accede   B. flail
    C. efface   D. annihilate

88. *spontaneous*   88.____

    A. hapless   B. corrosive
    C. intentional   D. willful

89. *disparage*   89.____

    A. abolish   B. exude   C. incriminate   D. extol

90. *timorous*   90.____

    A. succinct   B. chaste
    C. audacious   D. insouciant

KEY (CORRECT ANSWERS)

1.	D	21.	A	41.	A	61.	A	81.	B
2.	C	22.	B	42.	D	62.	B	82.	D
3.	B	23.	C	43.	C	63.	B	83.	B
4.	C	24.	B	44.	B	64.	C	84.	B
5.	C	25.	C	45.	A	65.	C	85.	C
6.	C	26.	C	46.	A	66.	B	86.	C
7.	B	27.	D	47.	D	67.	A	87.	A
8.	B	28.	B	48.	A	68.	C	88.	C
9.	A	29.	B	49.	C	69.	D	89.	D
10.	C	30.	C	50.	C	70.	A	90.	C
11.	C	31.	A	51.	B	71.	D		
12.	D	32.	B	52.	D	72.	C		
13.	C	33.	B	53.	C	73.	B		
14.	C	34.	D	54.	B	74.	A		
15.	A	35.	A	55.	D	75.	B		
16.	C	36.	B	56.	B	76.	B		
17.	A	37.	B	57.	C	77.	A		
18.	D	38.	D	58.	B	78.	D		
19.	B	39.	D	59.	B	79.	A		
20.	B	40.	A	60.	C	80.	C		

———

EXAMINATION SECTION
TEST 1

DIRECTIONS: In each of the following questions, only one of the four sentences conforms to standards of correct usage. The other three contain errors in grammar, diction, or punctuation. Select the choice in each question which BEST conforms to standards of correct usage. Consider a choice correct if it contains none of the errors mentioned above, even though there may be other ways of expressing the same thought. *PRINT THE LETTER OF THE CORRECT ANSWER IN THE SPACE AT THE RIGHT.*

1. A. Because he was ill was no excuse for his behavior.   1.____
    B. I insist that he see a lawyer before he goes to trial.
    C. He said "that he had not intended to go."
    D. He wasn't out of the office only three days.

2. A. He came to the station and pays a porter to carry his bags into the train.   2.____
    B. I should have liked to live in medieval times.
    C. My father was born in Linville. A little country town where everyone knows every-
        one else.
    D. The car, which is parked across the street, is disabled.

3. A. He asked the desk clerk for a clean, quiet, room.   3.____
    B. I expected James to be lonesome and that he would want to go home.
    C. I have stopped worrying because I have heard nothing further on the subject.
    D. If the board of directors controls the company, they may take actions which are dis-
        approved by the stockholders.

4. A. Each of the players knew their place.   4.____
    B. He whom you saw on the stage is the son of an actor.
    C. Susan is the smartest of the twin sisters.
    D. Who ever thought of him winning both prizes?

5. A. An outstanding trait of early man was their reliance on omens.   5.____
    B. Because I had never been there before.
    C. Neither Mr. Jones nor Mr. Smith has completed his work.
    D. While eating my dinner, a dog came to the window.

6. A. A copy of the lease, in addition to the Rules and Regulations, are to be given to   6.____
        each tenant.
    B. The Rules and Regulations and a copy of the lease is being given to each tenant.
    C. A copy of the lease, in addition to the Rules and Regulations, is to be given to each
        tenant.
    D. A copy of the lease, in addition to the Rules and Regulations, are being given to
        each tenant.

7. A. Although we understood that for him music was a passion, we were disturbed by   7.____
        the fact that he was addicted to sing along with the soloists.
    B. Do you believe that Steven is liable to win a scholarship?
    C. Give the picture to whomever is a connoisseur of art.
    D. Whom do you believe to be the most efficient worker in the office?

8.   A.   Each adult who is sure they know all the answers will some day realize their mistake.   8.____

        B.   Even the most hardhearted villain would have to feel bad about so horrible a tragedy.

        C.   Neither being licensed teachers, both aspirants had to pass rigorous tests before being appointed.

        D.   The principal reason why he wanted to be designated was because he had never before been to a convention.

9.   A.   Being that the weather was so inclement, the party has been postponed for at least a month.   9.____

        B.   He is in New York City only three weeks and he has already seen all the thrilling sights in Manhattan and in the other four boroughs.

        C.   If you will look it up in the official directory, which can be consulted in the library during specified hours, you will discover that the chairman and director are Mr. T. Henry Long.

        D.   Working hard at college during the day and at the post office during the night, he appeared to his family to be indefatigable.

10.   A.   I would have been happy to oblige you if you only asked me to do it.   10.____

        B.   The cold weather, as well as the unceasing wind and rain, have made us decide to spend the winter in Florida.

        C.   The politician would have been more successful in winning office if he would have been less dogmatic.

        D.   These trousers are expensive; however, they will wear well.

11.   A.   All except him wore formal attire at the reception for the ambassador.   11.____

        B.   If that chair were to be blown off of the balcony, it might injure someone below.

        C.   Not a passenger, who was in the crash, survived the impact.

        D.   To borrow money off friends is the best way to lose them.

12.   A.   Approaching Manhattan on the ferry boat from Staten Island, an unforgettable sight of the skyscrapers is seen.   12.____

        B.   Did you see the exhibit of modernistic paintings as yet?

        C.   Gesticulating wildly and ranting in stentorian tones, the speaker was the sinecure of all eyes.

        D.   The airplane with crew and passengers was lost somewhere in the Pacific Ocean.

13.   A.   If one has consistently had that kind of training, it is certainly too late to change your entire method of swimming long distances.   13.____

        B.   The captain would have been more impressed if you would have been more conscientious in evacuation drills.

        C.   The passengers on the stricken ship were all ready to abandon it at the signal.

        D.   The villainous shark lashed at the lifeboat with it's tail, trying to upset the rocking boat in order to partake of it's contents.

14. A. As one whose been certified as a professional engineer, I believe that the decision   14.____
to build a bridge over that harbor is unsound.
   B. Between you and me, this project ought to be completed long before winter arrives.
   C. He fervently hoped that the men would be back at camp and to find them busy at
their usual chores.
   D. Much to his surprise, he discovered that the climate of Korea was like his home
town.

15. A. An industrious executive is aided, not impeded, by having a hobby which gives him   15.____
a fresh point of view on life and its problems.
   B. Frequent absence during the calendar year will surely mitigate against the chances
of promotion.
   C. He was unable to go to the committee meeting because he was very ill.
   D. Mr. Brown expressed his disapproval so emphatically that his associates were
embarassed.

16. A. At our next session, the office manager will have told you something about his   16.____
duties and responsibilities.
   B. In general, the book is absorbing and original and have no hesitation about recommending it.
   C. The procedures followed by private industry in dealing with lateness and absence
are different from ours.
   D. We shall treat confidentially any information about Mr. Doe, to whom we understand you have sent reports to for many years.

17. A. I talked to one official, whom I knew was fully impartial.   17.____
   B. Everyone signed the petition but him.
   C. He proved not only to be a good student but also a good athlete.
   D. All are incorrect.

18. A. Every year a large amount of tenants are admitted to housing projects.   18.____
   B. Henry Ford owned around a billion dollars in industrial equipment.
   C. He was aggravated by the child's poor behavior.
   D. All are incorrect.

19. A. Before he was committed to the asylum he suffered from the illusion that he was   19.____
Napoleon.
   B. Besides stocks, there were also bonds in the safe.
   C. We bet the other team easily.
   D. All are incorrect.

20. A. Bring this report to your supervisor immediately.   20.____
   B. He set the chair down near the table.
   C. The capitol of New York is Albany.
   D. All are incorrect.

21. A. He was chosen to arbitrate the dispute because everyone knew he would be disin-   21.____
terested.
   B. It is advisable to obtain the best council before making an important decision.
   C. Less college students are interested in teaching than ever before.
   D. All are incorrect.

22. A. She, hearing a signal, the source lamp flashed.
    B. While hearing a signal, the source lamp flashed.
    C. In hearing a signal, the source lamp flashed.
    D. As she heard a signal, the source lamp flashed.

22._____

23. A. Every one of the time records have been initialed in the designated spaces.
    B. All of the time records has been initialed in the designated spaces.
    C. Each one of the time records was initialed in the designated spaces.
    D. The time records all been initialed in the designated spaces.

23._____

24. A. If there is no one else to answer the phone, you will have to answer it.
    B. You will have to answer it yourself if no one else answers the phone.
    C. If no one else is not around to pick up the phone, you will have to do it.
    D. You will have to answer the phone when nobodys here to do it.

24._____

25. A. Dr. Barnes not in his office. What could I do for you?
    B. Dr. Barnes is not in his office. Is there something I can do for you?
    C. Since Dr. Barnes is not in his office, might there be something I may do for you?
    D. Is there any ways I can assist you since Dr. Barnes is not in his office?

25._____

26. A. She do not understand how the new console works.
    B. The way the new console works, she doesn't understand.
    C. She doesn't understand how the new console works.
    D. The new console works, so that she doesn't understand.

26._____

27. A. Certain changes in family income must be reported as they occur.
    B. When certain changes in family income occur, it must be reported.
    C. Certain family income changes must be reported as they occur.
    D. Certain changes in family income must be reported as they have been occuring.

27._____

28. A. Each tenant has to complete the application themselves.
    B. Each of the tenants have to complete the application by himself.
    C. Each of the tenants has to complete the application himself.
    D. Each of the tenants has to complete the application by themselves.

28._____

29. A. Yours is the only building that the construction will effect.
    B. Your's is the only building affected by the construction.
    C. The construction will only effect your building.
    D. Yours is the only building that will be affected by the construction.

29._____

30. A. There is four tests left.
    B. The number of tests left are four.
    C. There are four tests left.
    D. Four of the tests remains.

30._____

31. A. Each of the applicants takes a test.
    B. Each of the applicants take a test.
    C. Each of the applicants take tests.
    D. Each of the applicants have taken tests.

31._____

32.
   A. The applicant, not the examiners, are ready.
   B. The applicants, not the examiner, is ready.
   C. The applicants, not the examiner, are ready.
   D. The applicant, not the examiner, are ready.

32.____

33.
   A. You will not progress except you practice.
   B. You will not progress without you practicing.
   C. You will not progress unless you practice.
   D. You will not progress provided you do not practice.

33.____

34.
   A. Neither the director or the employees will be at the office tomorrow.
   B. Neither the director nor the employees will be at the office tomorrow.
   C. Neither the director, or the secretary nor the other employees will be at the office tomorrow.
   D. Neither the director, the secretary or the other employees will be at the office tomorrow.

34.____

35.
   A. In my absence he and her will have to finish the assignment.
   B. In my absence he and she will have to finish the assignment.
   C. In my absence she and him, they will have to finish the assignment.
   D. In my absence he and her both will have to finish the assignment.

35.____

KEY (CORRECT ANSWERS)

1.	B		16.	C
2.	B		17.	B
3.	C		18.	D
4.	B		19.	B
5.	C		20.	B
6.	C		21.	A
7.	D		22.	D
8.	B		23.	C
9.	D		24.	A
10.	D		25.	B
11.	A		26.	C
12.	D		27.	A
13.	C		28.	C
14.	B		29.	D
15.	A		30.	C

31.	A
32.	C
33.	C
34.	B
35.	B

———

TEST 2

DIRECTIONS: Each question or incomplete statement is followed by several suggested answers or completions. Select the one that BEST answers the question or completes the statement. *PRINT THE LETTER OF THE CORRECT ANSWER IN THE SPACE AT THE RIGHT.*

Questions 1-4.

DIRECTIONS: Questions 1 through 4 consist of three sentences each. For each question, select the sentence which contains NO error in grammar or usage.

1. A. Be sure that everybody brings his notes to the conference.   1.____
   B. He looked like he meant to hit the boy.
   C. Mr. Jones is one of the clients who was chosen to represent the district
   D. All are incorrect.

2. A. He is taller than I.   2.____
   B. I'll have nothing to do with these kind of people.
   C. The reason why he will not buy the house is because it is too expensive.
   D. All are incorrect.

3. A. Aren't I eligible for this apartment.   3.____
   B. Have you seen him anywheres?
   C. He should of come earlier.
   D. All are incorrect.

4. A. He graduated college in 1982.   4.____
   B. He hadn't but one more line to write.
   C. Who do you think is the author of this report?
   D. All are incorrect.

Questions 5-35.

DIRECTIONS: In each of the following questions, only one of the four sentences conforms to standards of correct usage. The other three contain errors in grammar, diction, or punctuation. Select the choice in each question which BEST conforms to standards of correct usage. Consider a choice correct if it contains none of the errors mentioned above, even though there may be other ways of expressing the same thought.

5. A. It is obvious that no one wants to be a kill-joy if they can help it.   5.____
   B. It is not always possible, and perhaps it never ispossible, to judge a person's character by just looking at him.
   C. When Yogi Berra of the New York Yankees hit an immortal grandslam home run, everybody in the huge stadium including Pittsburgh fans, rose to his feet.
   D. Every one of us students must pay tuition today.

6.   A.   The physician told the young mother that if the baby is not able to digest its milk, it should be boiled.   6.____

       B.   There is no doubt whatsoever that he felt deeply hurt because John Smith had betrayed the trust.

       C.   Having partaken of a most delicious repast prepared by Tessie Breen, the hostess, the horses were driven home immediately thereafter.

       D.   The attorney asked my wife and myself several questions.

7.   A.   Despite all denials, there is no doubt in my mind that   7.____

       B.   At this time everyone must deprecate the demogogic attack made by one of our Senators on one of our most revered statesmen.

       C.   In the first game of a crucial two-game series, Ted Williams, got two singles, both of them driving in a run.

       D.   Our visitor brought good news to John and I.

8.   A.   If he would have told me, I should have been glad to help him in his dire financial emergency.   8.____

       B.   Newspaper men have often asserted that diplomats or so-called official spokes-men sometimes employ equivocation in attempts to deceive.

       C.   I think someones coming to collect money for the Red Cross.

       D.   In a masterly summation, the young attorney expressed his belief that the facts clearly militate against this opinion.

9.   A.   We have seen most all the exhibits.   9.____

       B.   Without in the least underestimating your advice, in my opinion the situation has grown immeasurably worse in the past few days.

       C.   I wrote to the box office treasurer of the hit show that a pair of orchestra seats would be preferable.

       D.   As the grim story of Pearl Harbor was broadcast on that fateful December 7, it was the general opinion that war was inevitable.

10.   A.   Without a moment's hesitation, Casey Stengel said that Larry Berra works harder than any player on the team.   10.____

       B.   There is ample evidence to indicate that many animals can run faster than any human being.

       C.   No one saw the accident but I.

       D.   Example of courage is the heroic defense put up by the paratroopers against over-whelming odds.

11.   A.   If you prefer these kind, Mrs. Grey, we shall be more than willing to let you have them reasonably.   11.____

       B.   If you like these here, Mrs. Grey, we shall be more than willing to let you have them reasonably.

       C.   If you like these, Mrs. Grey, we shall be more than willing to let you have them.

       D.   Who shall we appoint?

12.   A.   The number of errors are greater in speech than in writing.   12.____

       B.   The doctor rather than the nurse was to blame for his being neglected.

       C.   Because the demand for these books have been so great, we reduced the price.

       D.   John Galsworthy, the English novelist, could not have survived a serious illness; had it not been for loving care.

13.   A. Our activities this year have seldom ever been as interesting as they have been   13.____
this month.
     B. Our activities this month have been more interesting, or at least as interesting as those of any month this year.
     C. Our activities this month has been more interesting than those of any other month this year.
     D. Neither Jean nor her sister was at home.

14.   A. George B. Shaw's view of common morality, as well as his wit sparkling with a dash   14.____
of perverse humor here and there, have led critics to term him "The Incurable Rebel."
     B. The President's program was not always received with the wholehearted endorsement of his own party, which is why the party faces difficulty in drawing up a platform for the coming election.
     C. The reason why they wanted to travel was because they had never been away from home.
     D. Facing a barrage of cameras, the visiting celebrity found it extremely difficult to express his opinions clearly.

15.   A. When we calmed down, we all agreed that our anger had been kind of unneces-   15.____
sary and had not helped the situation.
     B. Without him going into all the details, he made us realize the horror of the accident.
     C. Like one girl, for example, who applied for two positions.
     D. Do not think that you have to be so talented as he is in order to play in the school orchestra.

16.   A. He looked very peculiarly to me.   16.____
     B. He certainly looked at me peculiar.
     C. Due to the train's being late, we had to wait an hour.
     D. The reason for the poor attendance is that it is raining.

17.   A. About one out of four own an automobile.   17.____
     B. The collapse of the old Mitchell Bridge was caused by defective construction in the central pier.
     C. Brooks Atkinson was well acquainted with the best literature, thus helping him to become an able critic.
     D. He has to stand still until the relief man comes up, thus giving him no chance to move about and keep warm.

18.   A. He is sensitive to confusion and withdraws from people whom he feels are too   18.____
noisy.
     B. Do you know whether the data is statistically correct?
     C. Neither the mayor or the aldermen are to blame.
     D. Of those who were graduated from high school, a goodly percentage went to college.

19.   A. Acting on orders, the offices were searched by a designated committee.   19.____
     B. The answer probably is nothing.
     C. I thought it to be all right to excuse them from class.
     D. I think that he is as successful a singer, if not more successful, than Mary.

20. A. $120,000 is really very little to pay for such a wellbuilt house.
     B. The creatures looked like they had come from outer space.
     C. It was her, he knew!
     D. Nobody but me knows what to do.

20.____

21. A. Mrs. Smith looked good in her new suit.
     B. New York may be compared with Chicago.
     C. I will not go to the meeting except you go with me.
     D. I agree with this editorial.

21.____

22. A. My opinions are different from his.
     B. There will be less students in class now.
     C. Helen was real glad to find her watch.
     D. It had been pushed off of her dresser.

22.____

23. A. Almost everone, who has been to California, returns with glowing reports.
     B. George Washington, John Adams, and Thomas Jefferson, were our first presi-
         dents.
     C. Mr. Walters, whom we met at the bank yesterday, is the man, who gave me my first
         job.
     D. One should study his lessons as carefully as he can.

23.____

24. A. We had such a good time yesterday.
     B. When the bell rang, the boys and girls went in the schoolhouse.
     C. John had the worst headache when he got up this morning.
     D. Today's assignment is somewhat longer than yesterday's.

24.____

25. A. Neither the mayor nor the city clerk are willing to talk.
     B. Neither the mayor nor the city clerk is willing to talk.
     C. Neither the mayor or the city clerk are willing to talk.
     D. Neither the mayor or the city clerk is willing to talk.

25.____

26. A. Being that he is that kind of boy, cooperation cannot be expected.
     B. He interviewed people who he thought had something to say.
     C. Stop whomever enters the building regardless of rank or office held.
     D. Passing through the countryside, the scenery pleased us.

26.____

27. A. The childrens' shoes were in their closet.
     B. The children's shoes were in their closet.
     C. The childs' shoes were in their closet.
     D. The childs' shoes were in his closet.

27.____

28. A. An agreement was reached between the defendant, the plaintiff, the plaintiff's
         attorney and the insurance company as to the amount of the settlement.
     B. Everybody was asked to give their versions of the accident.
     C. The consensus of opinion was that the evidence was inconclusive.
     D. The witness stated that if he was rich, he wouldn't have had to loan the money.

28.____

29.   A. Before beginning the investigation, all the materials relating to the case were carefully assembled.   29.____

       B. The reason for his inability to keep the appointment is because of his injury in the accident.

       C. This here evidence tends to support the claim of the defendant.

       D. We interviewed all the witnesses who, according to the driver, were still in town.

30.   A. Each claimant was allowed the full amount of their medical expenses.   30.____

       B. Either of the three witnesses is available.

       C. Every one of the witnesses was asked to tell his story.

       D. Neither of the witnesses are right.

31.   A. The commissioner, as well as his deputy and various bureau heads, were present.   31.____

       B. A new organization of employers and employees have been formed.

       C. One or the other of these men have been selected.

       D. The number of pages in the book is enough to discourage a reader.

32.   A. Between you and me, I think he is the better man.   32.____

       B. He was believed to be me.

       C. Is it us that you wish to see?

       D. The winners are him and her.

33.   A. Beside the statement to the police, the witness spoke to no one.   33.____

       B. He made no statement other than to the police and I.

       C. He made no statement to any one else, aside from the police.

       D. The witness spoke to no one but me.

34.   A. The claimant has no one to blame but himself.   34.____

       B. The boss sent us, he and I, to deliver the packages.

       C. The lights come from mine and not his car.

       D. There was room on the stairs for him and myself.

35.   A. Admission to this clinic is limited to patients' inability to pay for medical care.   35.____

       B. Patients who can pay little or nothing for medical care are treated in this clinic.

       C. The patient's ability to pay for medical care is the determining factor in his admissibility to this clinic.

       D. This clinic is for the patient's that cannot afford to pay or that can pay a little for medical care.

_____

KEY (CORRECT ANSWERS)

1.	A		16.	D
2.	A		17.	B
3.	D		18.	D
4.	C		19.	B
5.	D		20.	D
6.	D		21.	A
7.	B		22.	A
8.	B		23.	D
9.	D		24.	D
10.	B		25.	B
11.	C		26.	B
12.	B		27.	B
13.	D		28.	C
14.	D		29.	D
15.	D		30.	C

31.	D
32.	A
33.	D
34.	A
35.	B

EXAMINATION SECTION
TEST 1

DIRECTIONS: In each of the following tests in this part, select the letter of the one MIS-SPELLED word in each of the following groups of words. If no word is misspelled, select the last item, letter E (none misspelled). *PRINT THE LETTER OF THE CORRECT ANSWER IN THE SPACE AT THE RIGHT.*

1.   A. grateful   B. fundimental   C. census   1.____
      D. analysis   E. *NONE MISSPELLED*

2.   A. installment   B. retrieve   C. concede   2.____
      D. dissapear   E. *NONE MISSPELLED*

3.   A. accidentaly   B. dismissal   C. conscientious   3.____
      D. indelible   E. *NONE MISSPELLED*

4.   A. perceive   B. carreer   C. anticipate   4.____
      D. acquire   E. *NONE MISSPELLED*

5.   A. facility   B. reimburse   C. assortment   5.____
      D. guidance   E. *NONE MISSPELLED*

6.   A. plentiful   B. across   C. advantagous   6.____
      D. similar   E. *NONE MISSPELLED*

7.   A. omission   B. pamphlet   C. guarrantee   7.____
      D. repel   E. *NONE MISSPELLED*

8.   A. maintenance   B. always   C. liable   8.____
      D. anouncement   E. *NONE MISSPELLED*

9.   A. exaggerate   B. sieze   C. condemn   9.____
      D. commit   E. *NONE MISSPELLED*

10.   A. pospone   B. altogether   C. grievance   10.____
      D. excessive   E. *NONE MISSPELLED*

11.   A. arguing   B. correspondance   C. forfeit   11.____
      D. dissension   E. *NONE MISSPELLED*

12.   A. occasion   B. description   C. prejudice   12.____
      D. elegible   E. *NONE MISSPELLED*

13.   A. accomodate   B. initiative   C. changeable   13.____
      D. enroll   E. *NONE MISSPELLED*

14.   A. temporary   B. insistent   C. benificial   14.____
      D. separate   E. *NONE MISSPELLED*

15.   A. achieve   B. dissapoint   C. unanimous   15.____
      D. judgment   E. *NONE MISSPELLED*

16.   A. proceed   B. publicly   C. sincerity   16.____
      D. successful   E. *NONE MISSPELLED*

17.	A. deceive	B. goverment	C. preferable	17.____
	D. repetitive	E. *NONE MISSPELLED*		
18.	A. emphasis	B. skillful	C. advisible	18.____
	D. optimistic	E. *NONE MISSPELLED*		
19.	A. tendency	B. rescind	C. crucial	19.____
	D. noticable	E. *NONE MISSPELLED*		
20.	A. privelege	B. abbreviate	C. simplify	20.____
	D. divisible	E. *NONE MISSPELLED*		

KEY (CORRECT ANSWERS)

1. B. fundamental
2. D. disappear
3. A. accidentally
4. B. career
5. E. None Misspelled
6. C. advantageous
7. C. guarantee
8. D. announcement
9. B. seize
10. A. postpone
11. B. correspondence
12. D. eligible
13. A. accommodate
14. C. beneficial
15. B. disappoint
16. E. None Misspelled
17. B. government
18. C. advisable
19. D. noticeable
20. A. privilege

TEST 2

DIRECTIONS: In each of the following tests in this part, select the letter of the one MIS-SPELLED word in each of the following groups of words. If no word is mis-spelled, select the last item, letter E (none misspelled). *PRINT THE LETTER OF THE CORRECT ANSWER IN THE SPACE AT THE RIGHT.*

1. A. typical   B. descend   C. summarize   1.____
   D. continuel   E. *NONE MISSPELLED*

2. A. courageous   B. recomend   C. omission   2.____
   D. eliminate   E. *NONE MISSPELLED*

3. A. compliment   B. illuminate   C. auxilary   3.____
   D. installation   E. *NONE MISSPELLED*

4. A. preliminary   B. aquainted   C. syllable   4.____
   D. analysis   E. *NONE MISSPELLED*

5. A. accustomed   B. negligible   C. interupted   5.____
   D. bulletin   E. *NONE MISSPELLED*

6. A. summoned   B. managment   C. mechanism   6.____
   D. sequence   E. *NONE MISSPELLED*

7. A. commitee   B. surprise   C. noticeable   7.____
   D. emphasize   E. *NONE MISSPELLED*

8. A. occurrance   B. likely   C. accumulate   8.____
   D. grievance   E. grievance

9. A. obstacle   B. particuliar   C. baggage   9.____
   D. fascinating   E. *NONE MISSPELLED*

10. A. innumerable   B. seize   C. applicant   10.____
    D. dicionery   E. *NONE MISSPELLED*

11. A. primary   B. mechanic   C. referred   11.____
    D. admissible   E. *NONE MISSPELLED*

12. A. cessation   B. beleif   C. aggressive   12.____
    D. allowance   E. *NONE MISSPELLED*

13. A. leisure   B. authentic   C. familiar   13.____
    D. contemptable   E. *NONE MISSPELLED*

14. A. volume   B. forty   C. dilemma   14.____
    D. seldum   E. *NONE MISSPELLED*

15. A. discrepancy   B. aquisition   C. exorbitant   15.____
    D. lenient   E. *NONE MISSPELLED*

16. A. simultanous   B. penetrate   C. revision   16.____
    D. conspicuous   E. *NONE MISSPELLED*

17. A. ilegible   B. gracious   C. profitable   17.____
    D. obedience   E. *NONE MISSPELLED*

18.   A.   manufacturer   B.   authorize   C.   compelling   18._____
        D.   pecular   E.   *NONE MISSPELLED*

19.   A.   anxious   B.   rehearsal   C.   handicaped   19._____
        D.   tendency   E.   *NONE MISSPELLED*

20.   A.   meticulous   B.   accompaning   C.   initiative   20._____
        D.   shelves   E.   *NONE MISSPELLED*

KEY (CORRECT ANSWERS)

  1.   D.   continual
  2.   B.   recommend
  3.   C.   auxiliary
  4.   B.   acquainted
  5.   C.   interrupted
  6.   B.   management
  7.   A.   committee
  8.   A.   occurrence
  9.   B.   particular
10.   D.   dictionary
11.   E.   None Misspelled
12.   B.   belief
13.   D.   contemptible
14.   D.   seldom
15.   B.   acquisition
16.   A.   simultaneous
17.   A.   illegible
18.   D.   peculiar
19.   C.   handicapped
20.   B.   accompanying

TEST 3

DIRECTIONS: In each of the following tests in this part, select the letter of the one MIS-
SPELLED word in each of the following groups of words. If no word is mis-
spelled, select the last item, letter E (none misspelled). *PRINT THE LETTER
OF THE CORRECT ANSWER IN THE SPACE AT THE RIGHT.*

1.   A. grievous   B. dilettante   C. gibberish   1.____
     D. upbraid   E. *NONE MISSPELLED*

2.   A. embarrassing   B. playright   C. unmanageable   2.____
     D. symmetrical   E. *NONE MISSPELLED*

3.   A. sestet   B. denouement   C. liaison   3.____
     D. tattooing   E. *NONE MISSPELLED*

4.   A. prophesied   B. soliliquy   C. supersede   4.____
     D. hemorrhage   E. *NONE MISSPELLED*

5.   A. colossal   B. renascent   C. parallel   5.____
     D. omnivorous   E. *NONE MISSPELLED*

6.   A. passable   B. dispensable   C. deductable   6.____
     D. irreducible   E. *NONE MISSPELLED*

7.   A. guerrila   B. carousal   C. maneuver   7.____
     D. staid   E. *NONE MISSPELLED*

8.   A. maintenance   B. mountainous   C. sustenance   8.____
     D. gluttinous   E. *NONE MISSPELLED*

9.   A. holocaust   B. irascible   C. buccanneer   9.____
     D. mischievous   E. *NONE MISSPELLED*

10. A. diphthong   B. rhododendron   C. inviegle   10.____
     D. shellacked   E. *NONE MISSPELLED*

11. A. Phillipines   B. currant   C. dietitian   11.____
     D. coercion   E. *NONE MISSPELLED*

12. A. courtesey   B. buoyancy   C. fiery   12.____
     D. shepherd   E. *NONE MISSPELLED*

13. A. censor   B. queue   C. obbligato   13.____
     D. antartic   E. *NONE MISSPELLED*

14. A. chrystal   B. chrysanthemum   C. chrysalis   14.____
     D. chrome   E. *NONE MISSPELLED*

15. A. shreik   B. siege   C. sheik   15.____
     D. sieve   E. *NONE MISSPELLED*

16. A. leisure   B. gladioluses   C. kindergarden   16.____
     D. tonnage   E. *NONE MISSPELLED*

17. A. emminent   B. imminent   C. blatant   17.____
     D. privilege   E. *NONE MISSPELLED*

| 18. | A. | diphtheria | B. | collander | C. | seize | 18.___ |
| | D. | sleight | E. | *NONE MISSPELLED* | | | |

| 19. | A. | frolicking | B. | caramel | C. | germaine | 19.___ |
| | D. | kohlrabi | E. | *NONE MISSPELLED* | | | |

| 20. | A. | dispensable | B. | compatable | C. | recommend | 20.___ |
| | D. | feasible | E. | *NONE MISSPELLED* | | | |

KEY (CORRECT ANSWERS)

1. E. None Misspelled
2. B. playwright
3. E. None Misspelled
4. B. soliloquy
5. E. None Misspelled
6. C. deductible
7. A. guerrilla
8. D. gluttonous
9. C. buccaneer
10. C. inveigle
11. A. Philippines
12. A. courtesy
13. D. antarctic
14. A. crystal
15. A. shriek
16. C. kindergarten
17. A. eminent
18. B. colander
19. C. germane
20. B. compatible

TEST 4

DIRECTIONS: In each of the following tests in this part, select the letter of the one MIS-SPELLED word in each of the following groups of words. If no word is misspelled, select the last item, letter E (none misspelled). *PRINT THE LETTER OF THE CORRECT ANSWER IN THE SPACE AT THE RIGHT.*

1. A. coercion   B. rescission   C. license   1.____
    D. prophecied   E. *NONE MISSPELLED*

2. A. calcimine   B. seive   C. procedure   2.____
    D. poinsettia   E. *NONE MISSPELLED*

3. A. entymology   B. echoing   C. subtly   3.____
    D. stupefy   E. *NONE MISSPELLED*

4. A. mocassin   B. assassin   C. battalion   4.____
    D. despicable   E. *NONE MISSPELLED*

5. A. moustache   B. sovereignty   C. drunkeness   5.____
    D. staccato   E. *NONE MISSPELLED*

6. A. notoriety   B. stereotype   C. trellis   6.____
    D. Uraguay   E. *NONE MISSPELLED*

7. A. hummock   B. idiosyncrasy   C. licentiate   7.____
    D. plagiarism   E. *NONE MISSPELLED*

8. A. denim   B. hyssop   C. innoculate   8.____
    D. malevolent   E. *NONE MISSPELLED*

9. A. boundaries   B. corpulency   C. gauge   9.____
    D. jingoes   E. *NONE MISSPELLED*

10. A. assassin   B. refulgeant   C. sorghum   10.____
    D. suture   E. *NONE MISSPELLED*

11. A. dormatory   B. glimpse   C. mediocre   11.____
    D. repetition   E. *NONE MISSPELLED*

12. A. ambergris   B. docility   C. loquacious   12.____
    D. Pharoah   E. *NONE MISSPELLED*

13. A. curriculum   B. ninety-eighth   C. occurrence   13.____
    D. repertoire   E. *NONE MISSPELLED*

14. A. belladonna   B. equable   C. immersion   14.____
    D. naphtha   E. *NONE MISSPELLED*

15. A. itinerary   B. ptomaine   C. similar   15.____
    D. solicetous   E. *NONE MISSPELLED*

16. A. liquify   B. mausoleum   C. Philippines   16.____
    D. singeing   E. *NONE MISSPELLED*

17. A. descendant   B. harrassed   C. implausible   17.____
    D. irreverence   E. *NONE MISSPELLED*

18. A. crystallize   B. imperceptible   C. isinglass   18.____
     D. precede   E. *NONE MISSPELLED*

19. A. accommodate   B. deferential   C. gazeteer   19.____
     D. plenteous   E. *NONE MISSPELLED*

20. A. aching   B. buttress   C. indigenous   20.____
     D. mischievous   E. *NONE MISSPELLED*

KEY (CORRECT ANSWERS)

1. D. prophesied
2. B. sieve
3. A. entomology
4. A. moccasin
5. C. drunkenness
6. D. Uruguay
7. E. None Misspelled
8. C. inoculate
9. E. None Misspelled
10. B. refulgent
11. A. dormitory
12. D. Pharaoh
13. E. None Misspelled
14. E. None misspelled
15. D. solicitous
16. A. liquefy
17. B. harassed
18. E. None Misspelled
19. C. gazetteer
20. E. None Misspelled

TEST 5

DIRECTIONS: In each of the following tests in this part, select the letter of the one MIS-SPELLED word in each of the following groups of words. If no word is misspelled, select the last item, letter E (none misspelled). *PRINT THE LETTER OF THE CORRECT ANSWER IN THE SPACE AT THE RIGHT.*

1.   A. comensurable   B. fracas   C. obeisance   1.____
    D. remittent   E. *NONE MISSPELLED*

2.   A. defiance   B. delapidated   C. motley   2.____
    D. rueful   E. *NONE MISSPELLED*

3.   A. demeanor   B. epoch   C. furtive   3.____
    D. parley   E. *NONE MISSPELLED*

4.   A. disciples   B. influencial   C. nemesis   4.____
    D. poultry   E. *NONE MISSPELLED*

5.   A. decision   B. encourage   C. incidental   5.____
    D. satyr   E. *NONE MISSPELLED*

6.   A. collate   B. connivance   C. luxurient   6.____
    D. manageable   E. *NONE MISSPELLED*

7.   A. constituencies   B. crocheted   C. foreclosure   7.____
    D. scintillating   E. *NONE MISSPELLED*

8.   A. arraignment   B. assassination   C. carburator   8.____
    D. irrationally   E. *NONE MISSPELLED*

9.   A. livelihood   B. noticeable   C. optomiatic   9.____
    D. psychology   E. *NONE MISSPELLED*

10.   A. daub   B. massacre   C. repitition   10.____
    D. requiem   E. *NONE MISSPELLED*

11.   A. adversary   B. beneficiary   C. cemetery   11.____
    D. desultory   E. *NONE MISSPELLED*

12.   A. criterion   B. elicit   C. incredulity   12.____
    D. omnishient   E. *NONE MISSPELLED*

13.   A. dining   B. fiery   C. incidentally   13.____
    D. rheumatism   E. *NONE MISSPELLED*

14.   A. collaborator   B. gaudey   C. habilitation   14.____
    D. logician   E. *NONE MISSPELLED*

15.   A. dirge   B. ogle   C. recumbent   15.____
    D. reminiscence   E. *NONE MISSPELLED*

16.   A. conscientious   B. renunciation   C. inconvenient   16.____
    D. inoculate   E. *NONE MISSPELLED*

17.   A. crystalline   B. scimitar   C. ecstacy   17.____
    D. vestigial   E. *NONE MISSPELLED*

18.   A.   phlegmatic   B.   rhythm   C.   plebescite   18.____
       D.   refectory   E.   *NONE MISSPELLED*

19.   A.   resilient   B.   resevoir   C.   recipient   19.____
       D.   sobriety   E.   *NONE MISSPELLED*

20.   A.   privilege   B.   leige   C.   leisure   20.____
       D.   basilisk   E.   *NONE MISSPELLED*

KEY (CORRECT ANSWERS)

1.   A.   commensurable
2.   B.   dilapidated
3.   E.   None Misspelled
4.   B.   influential
5.   E.   None Misspelled
6.   C.   luxuriant
7.   E.   None Misspelled
8.   C.   carburetor
9.   C.   optimistic
10.   C.   repetition
11.   E.   None Misspelled
12.   D.   omniscient
13.   E.   None Misspelled
14.   B.   gaudy
15.   E.   None Misspelled
16.   E.   None Misspelled
17.   C.   ecstasy
18.   C.   plebiscite
19.   B.   reservoir
20.   B.   liege

TEST 6

DIRECTIONS: In each of the following tests in this part, select the letter of the one MIS-
SPELLED word in each of the following groups of words. If no word is mis-
spelled, select the last item, letter E (none misspelled). *PRINT THE LETTER
OF THE CORRECT ANSWER IN THE SPACE AT THE RIGHT.*

1. A. repellent   B. elliptical   C. paralelling   1.____
    D. colossal   E. *NONE MISSPELLED*

2. A. uproarious   B. grievous   C. armature   2.____
    D. tabular   E. *NONE MISSPELLED*

3. A. ammassed   B. embarrassed   C. promissory   3.____
    D. asymmetrical   E. *NONE MISSPELLED*

4. A. maintenance   B. correspondence   C. benificence   4.____
    D. miasmic   E. *NONE MISSPELLED*

5. A. demurred   B. occurrence   C. temperament   5.____
    D. abhorrance   E. *NONE MISSPELLED*

6. A. proboscis   B. lucious   C. mischievous   6.____
    D. vilify   E. *NONE MISSPELLED*

7. A. feasable   B. divisible   C. permeable   7.____
    D. forcible   E. *NONE MISSPELLED*

8. A. courteous   B. venemous   C. heterogeneous   8.____
    D. lustrous   E. *NONE MISSPELLED*

9. A. millionaire   B. mayonnaise   C. questionaire   9.____
    D. silhouette   E. *NONE MISSPELLED*

10. A. contemptible   B. irreverent   C. illimitable   10.____
    D. inveigled   E. *NONE MISSPELLED*

11. A. prevalent   B. irrelavent   C. ecstasy   11.____
    D. auxiliary   E. *NONE MISSPELLED*

12. A. impeccable   B. raillery   C. precede   12.____
    D. occurrence   E. *NONE MISSPELLED*

13. A. patrolling   B. vignette   C. ninety   13.____
    D. surveilance   E. *NONE MISSPELLED*

14. A. holocaust   B. incidently   C. weird   14.____
    D. canceled   E. *NONE MISSPELLED*

15. A. emmendation   B. gratuitous   C. fissionable   15.____
    D. dilemma   E. *NONE MISSPELLED*

16. A. harass   B. innuendo   C. capilary   16.____
    D. pachyderm   E. *NONE MISSPELLED*

17. A. concomitant   B. Lilliputian   C. sarcophagus   17.____
    D. melifluous   E. *NONE MISSPELLED*

18. A. interpolate   B. disident   C. venal   18.____
     D. inveigh   E. *NONE MISSPELLED*

19. A. supercillious   B. biennial   C. gargantuan   19.____
     D. irresistible   E. *NONE MISSPELLED*

20. A. conniving   B. expedite   C. inflammible   20.____
     D. incorruptible   E. *NONE MISSPELLED*

KEY (CORRECT ANSWERS)

1.	C.	paralleling
2.	E.	None Misspelled
3.	A.	amassed
4.	C.	beneficence
5.	D.	abhorrence
6.	B.	luscious
7.	A.	feasible
8.	B.	venomous
9.	C.	questionnaire
10.	E.	None Misspelled
11.	B.	irrelevant
12.	E.	None Misspelled
13.	D.	surveillance
14.	B.	incidentally
15.	A.	emendation
16.	C.	capillary
17.	D.	mellifluous
18.	B.	dissident
19.	A.	supercilious
20.	C.	inflammable

TEST 7

DIRECTIONS: In each of the following tests in this part, select the letter of the one MIS-
SPELLED word in each of the following groups of words. If no word is mis-
spelled, select the last item, letter E (none misspelled). *PRINT THE LETTER
OF THE CORRECT ANSWER IN THE SPACE AT THE RIGHT.*

1.	A. torturous D. flaccid	B. omniscient E. *NONE MISSPELLED*	C. hymenial	1.____
2.	A. seige D. grieve	B. seize E. *NONE MISSPELLED*	C. frieze	2.____
3.	A. indispensible D. receptacle	B. euphony E. *NONE MISSPELLED*	C. victuals	3.____
4.	A. schism D. epicurian	B. fortissimo E. *NONE MISSPELLED*	C. innocuous	4.____
5.	A. sustenance D. rarefy	B. vilefy E. *NONE MISSPELLED*	C. maintenance	5.____
6.	A. desiccated D. preponderance	B. alleviate E. *NONE MISSPELLED*	C. beneficence	6.____
7.	A. battalion D. innert	B. incubus E. *NONE MISSPELLED*	C. sacrilegious	7.____
8.	A. shiboleth D. dichotomy	B. connoisseur E. *NONE MISSPELLED*	C. potpourri	8.____
9.	A. pamphlet D. benefited	B. similar E. *NONE MISSPELLED*	C. parlament	9.____
10.	A. genealogy D. abhorrence	B. tyrannical E. *NONE MISSPELLED*	C. diletante	10.____
11.	A. effeminate D. fission	B. concensus E. *NONE MISSPELLED*	C. agglomeration	11.____
12.	A. narcissus D. peccadillo	B. lyceum E. *NONE MISSPELLED*	C. odissey	12.____
13.	A. stupefied D. frieze	B. psychiatry E. *NONE MISSPELLED*	C. onerous	13.____
14.	A. intelligible D. albumen	B. semaphore E. *NONE MISSPELLED*	C. pronounciation	14.____
15.	A. annihilate D. allergy	B. tyrannical E. *NONE MISSPELLED*	C. occurence	15.____
16.	A. gauging D. its	B. probossis E. *NONE MISSPELLED*	C. specimen	16.____
17.	A. diphthong D. dilemma	B. connoisseur E. *NONE MISSPELLED*	C. iresistible	17.____

18.	A. affect D. seize	B. baccillus E. *NONE MISSPELLED*	C. beige	18.____
19.	A. apostasy D. epigrammatic	B. sustenance E. *NONE MISSPELLED*	C. synonym	19.____
20.	A. discernable D. complement	B. consul E. *NONE MISSPELLED*	C. efflorescence	20.____

————

KEY (CORRECT ANSWERS)

1.	C.	hymeneal
2.	A.	siege
3.	A.	indispensable
4.	D.	epicurean
5.	B.	vilify
6.	E.	None Misspelled
7.	D.	inert
8.	A.	shibboleth
9.	C.	parliament
10.	C.	dilettante
11.	B.	consensus
12.	C.	odyssey
13.	E.	None Misspelled
14.	C.	pronunciation
15.	C.	occurrence
16.	B.	proboscis
17.	C.	irresistible
18.	B.	bacillus
19.	E.	None Misspelled
20.	A.	discernible

————

TEST 8

DIRECTIONS: In each of the following tests in this part, select the letter of the one MIS-
SPELLED word in each of the following groups of words. If no word is mis-
spelled, select the last item, letter E (none misspelled). *PRINT THE LETTER
OF THE CORRECT ANSWER IN THE SPACE AT THE RIGHT.*

1.   A.   righteous   B.   seafareing   C.   colloquial   1.____
     D.   contumely   E.   *NONE MISSPELLED*

2.   A.   sanitarium   B.   vicissitude   C.   mischievious   2.____
     D.   chlorophyll   E.   *NONE MISSPELLED*

3.   A.   captain   B.   theirs   C.   asceticism   3.____
     D.   acquiesced   E.   *NONE MISSPELLED*

4.   A.   across   B.   her's   C.   democracy   4.____
     D.   signature   E.   *NONE MISSPELLED*

5.   A.   villain   B.   vacillate   C.   imposter   5.____
     D.   temperament   E.   *NONE MISSPELLED*

6.   A.   idyllic   B.   volitile   C.   obloquy   6.____
     D.   emendation   E.   *NONE MISSPELLED*

7.   A.   heinous   B.   sattelite   C.   dissident   7.____
     D.   ephemeral   E.   *NONE MISSPELLED*

8.   A.   ennoble   B.   shellacked   C.   vilify   8.____
     D.   indissoluble   E.   *NONE MISSPELLED*

9.   A.   argueing   B.   intrepid   C.   papyrus   9.____
     D.   foulard   E.   *NONE MISSPELLED*

10. A.   guttural   B.   acknowleging   C.   isosceles   10.____
     D.   assonance   E.   *NONE MISSPELLED*

11. A.   shoeing   B.   exorcise   C.   development   11.____
     D.   irreperable   E.   *NONE MISSPELLED*

12. A.   counseling   B.   cancellation   C.   kidnapped   12.____
     D.   repellant   E.   *NONE MISSPELLED*

13. A.   disatisfy   B.   misstep   C.   usually   13.____
     D.   gregarious   E.   *NONE MISSPELLED*

14. A.   unparalleled   B.   beggar   C.   embarrass   14.____
     D.   ecstacy   E.   *NONE MISSPELLED*

15. A.   descendant   B.   poliomyelitis   C.   privilege   15.____
     D.   tragedy   E.   *NONE MISSPELLED*

16. A.   nullify   B.   siderial   C.   salability   16.____
     D.   irrelevant   E.   *NONE MISSPELLED*

17. A.   paraphenalia   B.   apothecaries   C.   occurrence   17.____
     D.   plagiarize   E.   *NONE MISSPELLED*

18. A. asinine   B. dissonent   C. opossum   18.____
     D. indispensable   E. *NONE MISSPELLED*

19. A. orifice   B. deferrment   C. harass   19.____
     D. accommodate   E. *NONE MISSPELLED*

20. A. changeable   B. therefor   C. incidently   20.____
     D. dissatisfy   E. *NONE MISSPELLED*

KEY (CORRECT ANSWERS)

1.	B.	seafaring
2.	C.	mischievous
3.	E.	None Misspelled
4.	B.	hers
5.	C.	impostor
6.	B.	volatile
7.	B.	satellite
8.	E.	None Misspelled
9.	A.	arguing
10.	B.	acknowledging
11.	D.	irreparable
12.	D.	repellent
13.	A.	dissatisfy
14.	D.	ecstasy
15.	E.	None Misspelled
16.	B.	sidereal
17.	A.	paraphernalia
18.	B.	dissonant
19.	B.	deferment
20.	C.	incidentally

TEST 9

DIRECTIONS: In each of the following tests in this part, select the letter of the one MIS-
SPELLED word in each of the following groups of words. If no word is mis-
spelled, select the last item, letter E (none misspelled). *PRINT THE LETTER
OF THE CORRECT ANSWER IN THE SPACE AT THE RIGHT.*

1. A. irreparably   B. lovable   C. comparitively   1.____
    D. audible   E. *NONE MISSPELLED*

2. A. vilify   B. efflorescence   C. sarcophagus   2.____
    D. sacreligious   E. *NONE MISSPELLED*

3. A. picnicking   B. proceedure   C. hypocrisy   3.____
    D. seize   E. *NONE MISSPELLED*

4. A. discomfit   B. sapient   C. exascerbate   4.____
    D. sarsaparilla   E. *NONE MISSPELLED*

5. A. valleys   B. maintainance   C. abridgment   5.____
    D. reticence   E. *NONE MISSPELLED*

6. A. idylic   B. beneficent   C. singeing   6.____
    D. asterisk   E. *NONE MISSPELLED*

7. A. appropos   B. violoncello   C. peony   7.____
    D. mucilage   E. *NONE MISSPELLED*

8. A. caterpillar   B. silhouette   C. rhapsody   8.____
    D. frieze   E. *NONE MISSPELLED*

9. A. appendicitis   B. vestigeal   C. colonnade   9.____
    D. tortuous   E. *NONE MISSPELLED*

10. A. omlet   B. diphtheria   C. highfalutin   10.____
    D. miniature   E. *NONE MISSPELLED*

11. A. diorama   B. sustanance   C. disastrous   11.____
    D. conscious   E. *NONE MISSPELLED*

12. A. inelegible   B. irreplaceable   C. dissatisfied   12.____
    D. procedural   E. *NONE MISSPELLED*

13. A. contemptible   B. sacrilegious   C. proffessor   13.____
    D. privilege   E. *NONE MISSPELLED*

14. A. inoculate   B. diptheria   C. gladioli   14.____
    D. hypocrisy   E. *NONE MISSPELLED*

15. A. pessimism   B. ecstasy   C. furlough   15.____
    D. vulnerible   E. *NONE MISSPELLED*

16. A. supersede   B. moccasin   C. recondite   16.____
    D. rhythmical   E. *NONE MISSPELLED*

17. A. Adirondack   B. Phillipines   C. Czechoslovakia   17.____
    D. Cincinnati   E. *NONE MISSPELLED*

| 18. | A. weird | B. impromptu | C. guerrila | 18.____ |
| | D. spontaneously | E. *NONE MISSPELLED* | | |

| 19. | A. newstand | B. accidentally | C. tangible | 19.____ |
| | D. reservoir | E. *NONE MISSPELLED* | | |

| 20. | A. macaroni | B. mackerel | C. ukulele | 20.____ |
| | D. giutar | E. *NONE MISSPELLED* | | |

KEY (CORRECT ANSWERS)

1.	C.	comparatively
2.	D.	sacrilegious
3.	B.	procedure
4.	C.	exacerbate
5.	B.	maintenance
6.	A.	idyllic
7.	A.	apropos
8.	E.	None Misspelled
9.	B.	vestigial
10.	A.	omelet
11.	B.	sustenance
12.	A.	ineligible
13.	C.	professor
14.	B.	diphtheria
15.	D.	vulnerable
16.	E.	None Misspelled
17.	B.	Philippines
18.	C.	guerrilla
19.	A.	newsstand
20.	D.	guitar

TEST 10

DIRECTIONS: In each of the following tests in this part, select the letter of the one MIS-
SPELLED word in each of the following groups of words. If no word is mis-
spelled, select the last item, letter E (none misspelled). *PRINT THE LETTER
OF THE CORRECT ANSWER IN THE SPACE AT THE RIGHT.*

1.   A. rescission   B. sacrament   C. hypocricy   1.____
     D. salable   E. *NONE MISSPELLED*

2.   A. rhythm   B. foreboding   C. withal   2.____
     D. consciousness   E. *NONE MISSPELLED*

3.   A. noticeable   B. drunkenness   C. frolicked   3.____
     D. abcess   E. *NONE MISSPELLED*

4.   A. supersede   B. canoeing   C. exorbitant   4.____
     D. vigilance   E. *NONE MISSPELLED*

5.   A. idiosyncrasy   B. pantomine   C. isosceles   5.____
     D. wintry   E. *NONE MISSPELLED*

6.   A. numbskull   B. indispensable   C. fatiguing   6.____
     D. gluey   E. *NONE MISSPELLED*

7.   A. dryly   B. egregious   C. recommend   7.____
     D. irresistable'   E. *NONE MISSPELLED*

8.   A. unforgettable   B. mackeral   C. perseverance   8.____
     D. rococo   E. *NONE MISSPELLED*

9.   A. mischievous   B. tyranical   C. desiccate   9.____
     D. battalion   E. *NONE MISSPELLED*

10. A. accede   B. ninth   C. abyssmal   10.____
     D. commonalty   E. *NONE MISSPELLED*

11. A. resplendent   B. colonnade   C. harass   11.____
     D. mimicking   E. *NONE MISSPELLED*

12. A. dilletante   B. pusillanimous   C. grievance   12.____
     D. cataclysm   E. *NONE MISSPELLED*

13. A. anomaly   B. connoisseur   C. feasable   13.____
     D. stationery   E. *NONE MISSPELLED*

14. A. ennervated   B. rescission   C. vacillate   14.____
     D. raucous   E. *NONE MISSPELLED*

15. A. liquefy   B. poniard   C. truculant   15.____
     D. weird   E. *NONE MISSPELLED*

16. A. existance   B. lieutenant   C. asinine   16.____
     D. parallelogram   E. *NONE MISSPELLED*

17. A. protuberant   B. nuisance   C. instrumental   17.____
     D. resevoir   E. *NONE MISSPELLED*

| 18. | A. | sustenance | B. | pedigree | C. | supercillious | 18.___ |
| | D. | clairvoyant | E. | *NONE MISSPELLED* | | | |

| 19. | A. | commingle | B. | bizarre | C. | gauge | 19.___ |
| | D. | priviledge | E. | *NONE MISSPELLED* | | | |

| 20. | A. | analagous | B. | irresistible | C. | apparel | 20.___ |
| | D. | hindrance | E. | *NONE MISSPELLED* | | | |

KEY (CORRECT ANSWERS)

1.	C.	hypocrisy
2.	E.	None Misspelled
3.	D.	abscess
4.	E.	None Misspelled
5.	B.	pantomime
6.	A.	numskull
7.	D.	irresistible
8.	B.	mackerel
9.	B.	tyrannical
10.	C.	abysmal
11.	E.	None Misspelled
12.	A.	dilettante
13.	C.	feasible
14.	A.	enervated
15.	C.	truculent
16.	A.	existence
17.	D.	reservoir
18.	C.	supercilious
19.	D.	privilege
20.	A.	analogous

TEST 11

DIRECTIONS: In each of the following tests in this part, select the letter of the one MIS-
SPELLED word in each of the following groups of words. If no word is mis-
spelled, select the last item, letter E (none misspelled). *PRINT THE LETTER
OF THE CORRECT ANSWER IN THE SPACE AT THE RIGHT.*

1.   A. impute   B. imparshal   C. immodest   1._____
     D. imminent   E. *NONE MISSPELLED*

2.   A. cover   B. audit   C. adege   2._____
     D. adder   E. *NONE MISSPELLED*

3.   A. promissory   B. maturity   C. severally   3._____
     D. accomodation   E. *NONE MISSPELLED*

4.   A. superintendant B. dependence   C. dependents   4._____
     D. entrance   E. *NONE MISSPELLED*

5.   A. managable   B. navigable   C. passable   5._____
     D. laughable   E. *NONE MISSPELLED*

6.   A. tolerance   B. circumference   C. insurance   6._____
     D. dominance   E. *NONE MISSPELLED*

7.   A. diameter   B. tangent   C. paralell   7._____
     D. perimeter   E. *NONE MISSPELLED*

8.   A. providential   B. personal   C. accidental   8._____
     D. diagonel   E. *NONE MISSPELLED*

9.   A. ballast   B. ballustrade   C. allotment   9._____
     D. bourgeois   E. *NONE MISSPELLED*

10. A. diverse   B. pedantic   C. mishapen   10._____
     D. transient   E. *NONE MISSPELLED*

11. A. surgeon   B. sturgeon   C. luncheon   11._____
     D. stancheon   E. *NONE MISSPELLED*

12. A. pariah   B. estrang   C. conceive   12._____
     D. puncilious   E. *NONE MISSPELLED*

13. A. camouflage   B. serviceable   C. mischievious   13._____
     D. menace   E. *NONE MISSPELLED*

14. A. forefeit   B. halve   C. hundredth   14._____
     D. illusion   E. *NONE MISSPELLED*

15. A. filial   B. arras   C. pantomine   15._____
     D. filament   E. *NONE MISSPELLED*

16. A. llama   B. madrigal   C. martinet   16._____
     D. laxitive   E. *NONE MISSPELLED*

17. A. symtom   B. serum   C. antiseptic   17._____
     D. aromatic   E. *NONE MISSPELLED*

18. A. erasable   B. irascible   C. audable   18.____
     D. laudable   E. *NONE MISSPELLED*

19. A. heroes   B. folios   C. sopranos   19.____
     D. cargos   E. *NONE MISSPELLED*

20. A. latent   B. goddess   C. aisle   20.____
     D. whose   E. *NONE MISSPELLED*

KEY (CORRECT ANSWERS)

        1.   B.   impartial
        2.   C.   adage
        3.   D.   accommodation
        4.   A.   superintendent
        5.   A.   manageable
        6.   E.   None Misspelled
        7.   C.   parallel
        8.   D.   diagonal
        9.   B.   balustrade
       10.   C.   misshapen
       11.   D.   stanchion
       12.   B.   estrange
       13.   C.   mischievous
       14.   A.   forfeit
       15.   C.   pantomime
       16.   D.   laxative
       17.   A.   symptom
       18.   C.   audible
       19.   D.   cargoes
       20.   E.   None Misspelled

TEST 12

DIRECTIONS: In each of the following tests in this part, select the letter of the one MIS-
SPELLED word in each of the following groups of words. If no word is mis-
spelled, select the last item, letter E (none misspelled). *PRINT THE LETTER
OF THE CORRECT ANSWER IN THE SPACE AT THE RIGHT.*

1.   A. coconut   B. bustling   C. abducter   1.____
     D. naphtha   E. *NONE MISSPELLED*

2.   A. seriatim   B. quadruped   C. diphthong   2.____
     D. concensus   E. *NONE MISSPELLED*

3.   A. sanction   B. propencity   C. parabola   3.____
     D. despotic   E. *NONE MISSPELLED*

4.   A. circumstantial   B. imbroglio   C. coalesce   4.____
     D. ductill   E. *NONE MISSPELLED*

5.   A. spontaneous   B. superlitive   C. telepathy   5.____
     D. thesis   E. *NONE MISSPELLED*

6.   A. adobe   B. apellate   C. billion   6.____
     D. chiropody   E. *NONE MISSPELLED*

7.   A. combatant   B. helium   C. esprit de corps   7.____
     D. debillity   E. *NONE MISSPELLED*

8.   A. iota   B. gopher   C. demoralize   8.____
     D. culvert   E. *NONE MISSPELLED*

9.   A. invideous   B. gourmand   C. embryo   9.____
     D. despicable   E. *NONE MISSPELLED*

10. A. dispeptic   B. dromedary   C. dormant   10.____
     D. duress   E. *NONE MISSPELLED*

11. A. spiggot   B. suffrage   C. technology   11.____
     D. thermostat   E. *NONE MISSPELLED*

12. A. aberration   B. antropology   C. bayou   12.____
     D. cashew   E. *NONE MISSPELLED*

13. A. ricochet   B. poncho   C. oposum   13.____
     D. melee   E. *NONE MISSPELLED*

14. A. semester   B. quadrent   C. penchant   14.____
     D. mustang   E. *NONE MISSPELLED*

15. A. rhetoric   B. polygimy   C. optimum   15.____
     D. mendicant   E. *NONE MISSPELLED*

16. A. labyrint   B. hegira   C. ergot   16.____
     D. debenture   E. *NONE MISSPELLED*

17. A. solvant   B. radioactive   C. photostat   17.____
     D. nominative   E. *NONE MISSPELLED*

| 18. | A. | sporadic | B. | excelsior | C. | tenible | 18.___ |
| | D. | thorax | E. | *NONE MISSPELLED* | | | |

| 19. | A. | mischievous | B. | bouillon | C. | asinine | 19.___ |
| | D. | alien | E. | *NONE MISSPELLED* | | | |

| 20. | A. | sanguinery | B. | prolix | C. | harangue | 20.___ |
| | D. | minutia | E. | *NONE MISSPELLED* | | | |

KEY (CORRECT ANSWERS)

1.	C.	abductor
2.	D.	consensus
3.	B.	propensity
4.	D.	ductile
5.	B.	superlative
6.	B.	appellate
7.	D.	debility
8.	E.	None Misspelled
9.	A.	invidious
10.	A.	dyspeptic
11.	A.	spigot
12.	B.	anthropology
13.	C.	opossum
14.	B.	quadrant
15.	B.	polygamy
16.	A.	labyrinth
17.	A.	solvent
18.	C.	tenable
19.	E.	None Misspelled
20.	A.	sanguinary

TEST 13

DIRECTIONS: In each of the following tests in this part, select the letter of the one MIS-
SPELLED word in each of the following groups of words. If no word is mis-
spelled, select the last item, letter E (none misspelled). *PRINT THE LETTER
OF THE CORRECT ANSWER IN THE SPACE AT THE RIGHT.*

1. A. controvert   B. cache   C. auricle   1.____
    D. impromptu   E. *NONE MISSPELLED*

2. A. labial   B. heffer   C. intrigue   2.____
    D. decagon   E. *NONE MISSPELLED*

3. A. statistics   B. syllable   C. tenon   3.____
    D. tituler   E. *NONE MISSPELLED*

4. A. lenient   B. migraine   C. embarras   4.____
    D. nepotism   E. *NONE MISSPELLED*

5. A. lichen   B. horoscope   C. orthadox   5.____
    D. pageant   E. *NONE MISSPELLED*

6. A. libretto   B. humis   C. fallacy   6.____
    D. dextrose   E. *NONE MISSPELLED*

7. A. clinical   B. alimoney   C. bourgeois   7.____
    D. proverbial   E. *NONE MISSPELLED*

8. A. dictator   B. clipper   C. braggadoccio   8.____
    D. assuage   E. *NONE MISSPELLED*

9. A. reverence   B. hydraulic   C. felon   9.____
    D. diaphram   E. *NONE MISSPELLED*

10. A. retrobution   B. polyp   C. optician   10.____
    D. mentor   E. *NONE MISSPELLED*

11. A. resonant   B. helicopter   C. rejoicing   11.____
    D. decisive   E. *NONE MISSPELLED*

12. A. renigade   B. restitution   C. faculty   12.____
    D. devise   E. *NONE MISSPELLED*

13. A. solicitors   B. gratuitous   C. spherical   13.____
    D. crusible   E. *NONE MISSPELLED*

14. A. spongy   B. ramify   C. pica   14.____
    D. noxtious   E. *NONE MISSPELLED*

15. A. automaton   B. cadence   C. consummate   15.____
    D. ancillery   E. *NONE MISSPELLED*

16. A. magnanimous   B. iminent   C. tonsillitis   16.____
    D. dowager   E. *NONE MISSPELLED*

17. A. aerial   B. apprehend   C. bilinear   17.____
    D. transum   E. *NONE MISSPELLED*

18.   A.   vacuum   B.   idiom   C.   veriety   18.____
       D.   warbler   E.   *NONE MISSPELLED*

19.   A.   zephyr   B.   rarify   C.   physiology   19.____
       D.   nonpareil   E.   *NONE MISSPELLED*

20.   A.   risque   B.   posterity   C.   opus   20.____
       D.   meridian   E.   *NONE MISSPELLED*

_____

KEY (CORRECT ANSWERS)

1.   E.   None Misspelled
2.   B.   heifer
3.   D.   titular
4.   C.   embarrass
5.   C.   orthodox
6.   B.   humus
7.   B.   alimony
8.   C.   braggadocio
9.   D.   diaphragm
10.   A.   retribution
11.   E.   None Misspelled
12.   A.   renegade
13.   D.   crucible
14.   D.   noxious
15.   D.   ancillary
16.   B.   imminent
17.   D.   transom
18.   C.   variety
19.   B.   rarefy
20.   D.   meridian

_____

TEST 14

DIRECTIONS: In each of the following tests in this part, select the letter of the one MIS-SPELLED word in each of the following groups of words. If no word is mis-spelled, select the last item, letter E (none misspelled). *PRINT THE LETTER OF THE CORRECT ANSWER IN THE SPACE AT THE RIGHT.*

1. A. pygmy   B. seggregation   C. clayey   1._____
    D. homogeneous   E. *NONE MISSPELLED*

2. A. homeopathy   B. predelection   C. hindrance   2._____
    D. guillotine   E. *NONE MISSPELLED*

3. A. cumulative   B. dandelion   C. incission   3._____
    D. malpractice   E. *NONE MISSPELLED*

4. A. paradise   B. allegiance   C. frustrate   4._____
    D. impecunious   E. *NONE MISSPELLED*

5. A. licquor   B. mousse   C. exclamatory   5._____
    D. disciple   E. *NONE MISSPELLED*

6. A. lame   B. winesome   C. valvular   6._____
    D. unadvised   E. *NONE MISSPELLED*

7. A. Terre Haute   B. Cyrano de Bergerac   C. Stamboul   7._____
    D. Roosvelt   E. *NONE MISSPELLED*

8. A. perambulator   B. ruminate   C. litturgy   8._____
    D. staple   E. *NONE MISSPELLED*

9. A. hectic   B. inpregnate   C. otter   9._____
    D. muscat   E. *NONE MISSPELLED*

10. A. lighterage   B. lumbar   C. insurence   10._____
    D. monsoon   E. *NONE MISSPELLED*

11. A. lethal   B. iliterateness   C. manifold   11._____
    D. minuet   E. *NONE MISSPELLED*

12. A. forfeit   B. halve   C. hundredth   12._____
    D. illusion   E. *NONE MISSPELLED*

13. A. dissolute   B. conundrum   C. fallacious   13._____
    D. descrimination   E. *NONE MISSPELLED*

14. A. diva   B. codicile   C. expedient   14._____
    D. garrison   E. *NONE MISSPELLED*

15. A. filial   B. arras   C. pantomine   15._____
    D. filament   E. *NONE MISSPELLED*

16. A. inveigle   B. paraphenalia   C. archivist   16._____
    D. complexion   E. *NONE MISSPELLED*

17. A. dessicate   B. ambidextrous   C. meritorious   17._____
    D. revocable   E. *NONE MISSPELLED*

18.	A. queue D. binnocular	B. isthmus E. *NONE MISSPELLED*	C. committal	18.___
19.	A. changeable D. japanned	B. abbreviating E. *NONE MISSPELLED*	C. regretable	19.___
20.	A. Saskechewan D. Apennines	B. Bismarck E. *NONE MISSPELLED*	C. Albuquerque	20.___

KEY (CORRECT ANSWERS)

1.	B.	segregation
2.	B.	predilection
3.	C.	incision
4.	E.	None Misspelled
5.	A.	liquor
6.	B.	winsome
7.	D.	Roosevelt
8.	C.	liturgy
9.	B.	impregnate
10.	C.	insurance
11.	B.	illiterateness
12.	E.	None Misspelled
13.	D.	discrimination
14.	B.	codicil
15.	C.	pantomime
16.	B.	paraphernalia
17.	A.	desiccate
18.	D.	binocular
19.	C.	regrettable
20.	A.	Saskatchewan

TEST 15

DIRECTIONS: In each of the following tests in this part, select the letter of the one MIS-
SPELLED word in each of the following groups of words. If no word is mis-
spelled, select the last item, letter E (none misspelled). *PRINT THE LETTER
OF THE CORRECT ANSWER IN THE SPACE AT THE RIGHT.*

1. A. culinery   B. millinery   C. humpbacked   1.____
    D. improvise   E. *NONE MISSPELLED*

2. A. Brittany   B. embarrassment   C. coifure   2.____
    D. leveled   E. *NONE MISSPELLED*

3. A. minnion   B. aborgine   C. antagonism   3.____
    D. arabesque   E. *NONE MISSPELLED*

4. A. tractible   B. camouflage   C. permanent   4.____
    D. dextrous   E. *NONE MISSPELLED*

5. A. inequitous   B. kilowatt   C. weasel   5.____
    D. lunging   E. *NONE MISSPELLED*

6. A. palatable   B. odious   C. motif   6.____
    D. Maltese   E. *NONE MISSPELLED*

7. A. Beau Brummel   B. Febuary   C. Bedouin   7.____
    D. Damascus   E. *NONE MISSPELLED*

8. A. llama   B. madrigal   C. illitive   8.____
    D. marlin   E. *NONE MISSPELLED*

9. A. babboon   B. dossier   C. esplanade   9.____
    D. frontispiece   E. *NONE MISSPELLED*

10. A. thrashing   B. threshing   C. atavism   10.____
    D. artifect   E. *NONE MISSPELLED*

11. A. ballast   B. ballustrade   C. allotment   11.____
    D. bourgeois   E. *NONE MISSPELLED*

12. A. amenuensis   B. saccharine   C. hippopotamus   12.____
    D. rhinoceros   E. *NONE MISSPELLED*

13. A. maintenance   B. bullion   C. khaki   13.____
    D. libarian   E. *NONE MISSPELLED*

14. A. diverse   B. pedantic   C. mishapen   14.____
    D. transient   E. *NONE MISSPELLED*

15. A. exhilirate   B. avaunt   C. avocado   15.____
    D. avocation   E. *NONE MISSPELLED*

16. A. narcotic   B. flippancy   C. daffodil   16.____
    D. narcisus   E. *NONE MISSPELLED*

17. A. inflamation   B. disfranchisement   C. surmise   17.____
    D. adviser   E. *NONE MISSPELLED*

| 18. | A. syphon | B. inquiry | C. shanghaied | 18.____ |
| | D. collapsible | E. *NONE MISSPELLED* | | |

| 19. | A. occassionally | B. antecedence | C. reprehensible | 19.____ |
| | D. inveigh | E. *NONE MISSPELLED* | | |

| 20. | A. crescendos | B. indispensible | C. mosquitoes | 20.____ |
| | D. impeccable | E. *NONE MISSPELLED* | | |

KEY (CORRECT ANSWERS)

1. A. culinary
2. C. coiffure
3. A. minion
4. A. tractable
5. A. iniquitous
6. E. None Misspelled
7. B. February
8. D. illative
9. A. baboon
10. D. artifact
11. B. balustrade
12. A. amanuensis
13. D. librarian
14. C. misshapen
15. A. exhilarate
16. D. narcissus
17. A. inflammation
18. E. None Misspelled
19. A. occasionally
20. B. indispensable

READING COMPREHENSION
UNDERSTANDING AND INTERPRETING WRITTEN MATERIAL
EXAMINATION SECTION
TEST 1

DIRECTIONS: Each question or incomplete statement is followed by several suggested answers or completions. Select the one that BEST answers the question or completes the statement. *PRINT THE LETTER OF THE CORRECT ANSWER IN THE SPACE AT THE RIGHT.*

Questions 1-3.

DIRECTIONS: Questions 1 through 3 are to be answered SOLELY on the basis of the following statement.

The equipment in a mailroom may include a mail metering machine. This machine simultaneously stamps, postmarks, seals, and counts letters as fast as the operator can feed them. It can also print the proper postage directly on a gummed strip to be affixed to bulky items. It is equipped with a meter which is removed from the machine and sent to the postmaster to be set for a given number of stampings of any denomination. The setting of the meter must be paid for in advance. One of the advantages of metered mail is that it bypasses the cancellation operation and thereby facilitates handling by the post office. Mail metering also makes the pilfering of stamps impossible, but does not prevent the passage of personal mail in company envelopes through the meters unless there is established a rigid control or censorship over outgoing mail.

1. According to this statement, the postmaster   1.____

    A. is responsible for training new clerks in the use of mail metering machines
    B. usually recommends that both large and small firms adopt the use of mail metering machines
    C. is responsible for setting the meter to print a fixed number of stampings
    D. examines the mail metering machine to see that they are properly installed in the mailroom

2. According to this statement, the use of mail metering machines   2.____

    A. requires the employment of more clerks in a mailroom than does the use of postage stamps
    B. interferes with the handling of large quantities of outgoing mail
    C. does not prevent employees from sending their personal letters at company expense
    D. usually involves smaller expenditures for mailroom equipment than does the use of postage stamps

3. On the basis of this statement, it is MOST accurate to state that   3.____

    A. mail metering machines are often used for opening envelopes
    B. postage stamps are generally used when bulky packages are to be mailed
    C. the use of metered mail tends to interfere with rapid mail handling by the post office
    D. mail metering machines can seal and count letters at the same time

Questions 4-5.

DIRECTIONS: Questions 4 and 5 are to be answered SOLELY on the basis of the following
                        statement.

Forms are printed sheets of paper on which information is to be entered. While what is
printed on the form is most important, the kind of paper used in making the form is also
important. The kind of paper should be selected with regard to the use to which the form will
be subjected. Printing a form on an unnecessarily expensive grade of papers is wasteful. On
the other hand, using too cheap or flimsy a form can materially interfere with satisfactory performance of the work the form is being planned to do. Thus, a form printed on both sides normally requires a heavier paper than a form printed only on one side. Forms to be used as
permanent records, or which are expected to have a very long life in files, requires a quality of
paper which will not disintegrate or discolor with age. A form which will go through a great
deal of handling requires a strong, tough paper, while thinness is a necessary qualification
where the making of several copies of a form will be required.

4.   According to this statement, the type of paper used for making forms   4.____

    A.   should be chosen in accordance with the use to which the form will be put
    B.   should be chosen before the type of printing to be used has been decided upon
    C.   is as important as the information which is printed on it
    D.   should be strong enough to be used for any purpose

5.   According to this statement, forms that are   5.____

    A.   printed on both sides are usually economical and desirable
    B.   to be filed permanently should not deteriorate as time goes on
    C.   expected to last for a long time should be handled carefully
    D.   to be filed should not be printed on inexpensive paper

Questions 6-8.

DIRECTIONS: Questions 6 through 8 are to be answered SOLELY on the basis of the follow-
                        ing paragraph.

The increase in the number of public documents in the last two centuries closely
matches the increase in population in the United States. The great number of public documents has become a serious threat to their usefulness. It is necessary to have programs
which will reduce the number of public documents that are kept and which will, at the same
time, assure keeping those that have value. Such programs need a great deal of thought to
have any success.

6.   According to the above paragraph, public documents may be LESS useful if   6.____

    A.   the files are open to the public
    B.   the record room is too small
    C.   the copying machine is operated only during normal working hours
    D.   too many records are being kept

7. According to the above paragraph, the growth of the population in the United States has matched the growth in the quantity of public documents for a period of MOST NEARLY _____ years.

    A. 50   B. 100   C. 200   D. 300

7.____

8. According to the above paragraph, the increased number of public documents has made it necessary to

    A. find out which public documents are worth keeping
    B. reduce the great number of public documents by decreasing government services
    C. eliminate the copying of all original public documents
    D. avoid all new copying devices

8.____

Questions 9-10.

DIRECTIONS: Questions 9 and 10 are to be answered SOLELY on the basis of the following paragraph.

The work goals of an agency can best be reached if the employees understand and agree with these goals. One way to gain such understanding and agreement is for management to encourage and seriously consider suggestions from employees in the setting of agency goals.

9. On the basis of the above paragraph, the BEST way to achieve the work goals of an agency is to

    A. make certain that employees work as hard as possible
    B. study the organizational structure of the agency
    C. encourage employees to think seriously about the agency's problems
    D. stimulate employee understanding of the work goals

9.____

10. On the basis of the above paragraph, understanding and agreement with agency goals can be gained by

    A. allowing the employees to set agency goals
    B. reaching agency goals quickly
    C. legislative review of agency operations
    D. employee participation in setting agency goals

10.____

Questions 11-13.

DIRECTIONS: Questions 11 through 13 are to be answered SOLELY on the basis of the following paragraph.

In order to organize records properly, it is necessary to start from their very beginning and trace each copy of the record to find out how it is used, how long it is used, and what may finally be done with it. Although several copies of the record are made, one copy should be marked as the copy of record. This is the formal legal copy, held to meet the requirements of the law. The other copies may be retained for brief periods for reference purposes, but these copies should not be kept after their usefulness as reference ends. There is another reason for tracing records through the office and that is to determine how long it takes the copy of record to reach the central file. The copy of record must not be kept longer than necessary by the section of the office which has prepared it, but should be sent to the central file as soon as possible so that it can be available to the various sections of the office. The central file can make the copy of record available to the various sections of the office at an early date only if it arrives at the central file as quickly as possible. Just as soon as its immediate or active service period is ended, the copy of record should be removed from the central file and put into the inactive file in the office to be stored for whatever length of time may be necessary to meet legal requirements, and then destroyed.

11. According to the above paragraph, a reason for tracing records through an office is to   11.____

A. determine how long the central file must keep the records
B. organize records properly
C. find out how many copies of each record are required
D. identify the copy of record

12. According to the above paragraph, in order for the central file to have the copy of record   12.____
available as soon as possible for the various sections of the office, it is MOST important that the

A. copy of record to be sent to the central file meets the requirements of the law
B. copy of record is not kept in the inactive file too long
C. section preparing the copy of record does not unduly delay in sending it to the central file
D. central file does not keep the copy of record beyond its active service period

13. According to the above paragraph, the length of time a copy of a record is kept in the   13.____
inactive file of an office depends CHIEFLY on the

A. requirements of the law
B. length of time that is required to trace the copy of record through the office
C. use that is made of the copy of record
D. length of the period that the copy of record is used for reference purposes

Questions 14-16.

DIRECTIONS: Questions 14 through 16 are to be answered SOLELY on the basis of the following paragraph.

The office was once considered as nothing more than a focal point of internal and external correspondence. It was capable only of dispatching a few letters upon occasion and of preparing records of little practical value. Under such a concept, the vitality of the office force was impaired. Initiative became stagnant, and the lot of the office worker was not likely to be a happy one. However, under the new concept of office management, the possibilities of waste and mismanagement in office operation are now fully recognized, as are the possibilities for the modern office to assist in the direction and control of business operations. Fortunately, the modern concept of the office as a centralized service-rendering unit is gaining ever greater acceptance in today's complex business world, for without the modern office, the production wheels do not turn and the distribution of goods and services is not possible.

14. According to the above paragraph, the fundamental difference between the old and the new concept of the office is the change in the

    A. accepted functions of the office
    B. content and the value of the records kept
    C. office methods and systems
    D. vitality and morale of the office force

14.____

15. According to the above paragraph, an office operated today under the old concept of the office MOST likely would

    A. make older workers happy in their jobs
    B. be part of an old thriving business concern
    C. have a passive role in the conduct of a business enterprise
    D. attract workers who do not believe in modern methods

15.____

16. Of the following, the MOST important implication of the above paragraph is that a present-day business organization cannot function effectively without the

    A. use of modern office equipment
    B. participation and cooperation of the office
    C. continued modernization of office procedures
    D. employment of office workers with skill and initiative

16.____

Questions 17-20.

DIRECTIONS: Questions 17 through 20 are to be answered SOLELY on the basis of the following paragraph.

A report is frequently ineffective because the person writing it is not fully acquainted with all the necessary details before he actually starts to construct the report. All details pertaining to the subject should be known before the report is started. If the essential facts are not known, they should be investigated. It is wise to have essential facts written down rather than to depend too much on memory, especially if the facts pertain to such matters as amounts, dates, names of persons, or other specific data. When the necessary information has been gathered, the general plan and content of the report should be thought out before the writing is actually begun. A person with little or no experience in writing reports may find that it is wise to make a brief outline. Persons with more experience should not need a written outline, but they should make mental notes of the steps they are to follow. If writing reports without dictation is a regular part of an office worker's duties, he should set aside a certain time during the day when he is least likely to be interrupted. That may be difficult, but in most offices there are certain times in the day when the callers, telephone calls, and other interruptions are not numerous. During those times, it is best to write reports that need undivided concentration. Reports that are written amid a series of interruptions may be poorly done.

17. Before starting to write an effective report, it is necessary to

    A. memorize all specific information
    B. disregard ambiguous data
    C. know all pertinent information
    D. develop a general plan

17.____

18. Reports dealing with complex and difficult material should be   18.____

    A. prepared and written by the supervisor of the unit
    B. written when there is the least chance of interruption
    C. prepared and written as part of regular office routine
    D. outlined and then dictated

19. According to the paragraph, employees with no prior familiarity in writing reports may find   19.____
it helpful to

    A. prepare a brief outline
    B. mentally prepare a synopsis of the report's content
    C. have a fellow employee help in writing the report
    D. consult previous reports

20. In writing a report, needed information which is unclear should be   20.____

    A. disregarded   B. memorized
    C. investigated   D. gathered

Questions 21-25.

DIRECTIONS: Questions 21 through 25 are to be answered SOLELY on the basis of the following passage.

Positive discipline minimizes the amount of personal supervision required and aids in the
maintenance of standards. When a new employee has been properly introduced and carefully instructed, when he has come to know the supervisor and has confidence in the supervisor's ability to take care of him, when he willingly cooperates with the supervisor, that
employee has been under positive discipline and can be put on his own to produce the quantity and quality of work desired. Negative discipline, the fear of transfer to a less desirable location, for example, to a limited extent may restrain certain individuals from overt violation of
rules and regulations governing attendance and conduct which in governmental agencies are
usually on at least an agency-wide basis. Negative discipline may prompt employees to perform according to certain rules to avoid a penalty such as, for example, docking for tardiness.

21. According to the above passage, it is reasonable to assume that in the area of discipline,   21.____
the first-line supervisor in a governmental agency has GREATER scope for action in

    A. *positive* discipline, because negative discipline is largely taken care of by agency
rules and regulations
    B. *negative* discipline, because rules and procedures are already fixed and the super-
visor can rely on them
    C. *positive* discipline, because the supervisor is in a position to recommend transfers
    D. *negative* discipline, because positive discipline is reserved for people on a higher
supervisory level

22. In order to maintain positive discipline of employees under his supervision, it is MOST   22.____
important for a supervisor to

    A. assure each employee that he has nothing to worry about
    B. insist at the outset on complete cooperation from employees

C. be sure that each employee is well trained in his job
D. inform new employees of the penalties for not meeting standards

23. According to the above passage, a feature of negative discipline is that it   23.____

   A. may lower employee morale
   B. may restrain employees from disobeying the rules
   C. censures equal treatment of employees
   D. tends to create standards for quality of work

24. A REASONABLE conclusion based on the above passage is that positive discipline ben-   24.____
    efits a supervisor because

   A. he can turn over orientation and supervision of a new employee to one of his sub-
      ordinates
   B. subordinates learn to cooperate with one another when working on an assignment
   C. it is easier to administer
   D. it cuts down, in the long run, on the amount of time the supervisor needs to spend
      on direct supervision

25. Based on the above passage, it is REASONABLE to assume, that an important differ-   25.____
    ence between positive discipline and negative discipline is that positive discipline

   A. is concerned with the quality of work and negative discipline with the quantity of
      work
   B. leads to a more desirable basis for motivation of the employee
   C. is more likely to be concerned with agency rules and regulations
   D. uses fear while negative discipline uses penalties to prod employees to adequate
      performance

KEY (CORRECT ANSWERS)

1.	C	11.	B
2.	C	12.	C
3.	D	13.	A
4.	A	14.	A
5.	B	15.	C
6.	D	16.	B
7.	C	17.	C
8.	A	18.	B
9.	D	19.	A
10.	D	20.	B

21.	A
22.	C
23.	B
24.	D
25.	B

TEST 2

Questions 1-6.

DIRECTIONS: Questions 1 through 6 are to be answered SOLELY on the basis of the following passage.

Inherent in all organized endeavors is the need to resolve the individual differences involved in conflict. Conflict may be either a positive or negative factor since it may lead to creativity, innovation and progress on the one hand, or it may result, on the other hand, in a deterioration or even destruction of the organization. Thus, some forms of conflict are desirable, whereas others are undesirable and ethically wrong.

There are three management strategies which deal with interpersonal conflict. In the *divide-and-rule strategy,* management attempts to maintain control by limiting the conflict to those directly involved and preventing their disagreement from spreading to the larger group. The *suppression-of-differences strategy* entails ignoring conflicts or pretending they are irrelevant. In the *working-through-differences strategy,* management actively attempts to solve or resolve intergroup or interpersonal conflicts. Of the three strategies, only the last directly attacks and has the potential for eliminating the causes of conflict. An essential part of this strategy, however, is its employment by a committed and relatively mature management team.

1. According to the above passage, the *divide-and-rule strategy tor* dealing with conflict is the attempt to   1.____

   A. involve other people in the conflict
   B. restrict the conflict to those participating in it
   C. divide the conflict into positive and negative factors
   D. divide the conflict into a number of smaller ones

2. The word *conflict* is used in relation to both positive and negative factors in this passage. Which one of the following words is MOST likely to describe the activity which the word *conflict,* in the sense of the passage, implies?   2.____

   A. Competition   B. Confusion
   C. Cooperation   D. Aggression

3. According to the above passage, which one of the following characteristics is shared by both the *suppression-of-differences strategy* and the *divide-and-rule strategy?*   3.____

   A. Pretending that conflicts are irrelevant
   B. Preventing conflicts from spreading to the group situation
   C. Failure to directly attack the causes of conflict
   D. Actively attempting to resolve interpersonal conflict

4. According to the above passage, the successful resolution of interpersonal conflict requires   4.____

   A. allowing the group to mediate conflicts between two individuals
   B. division of the conflict into positive and negative factors
   C. involvement of a committed, mature management team
   D. ignoring minor conflicts until they threaten the organization

5. Which can be MOST reasonably inferred from the above passage? Conflict between two   5.____
   individuals is LEAST likely to continue when management uses

   A. the *working-through differences strategy*
   B. the *suppression-of differences strategy*
   C. the *divide-and-rule strategy*
   D. a combination of all three strategies

6. According to the above passage, a DESIRABLE result of conflict in an organization is   6.____
   when conflict

   A. exposes production problems in the organization
   B. can be easily ignored by management
   C. results in advancement of more efficient managers
   D. leads to development of new methods

Questions 7-13.

DIRECTIONS: Questions 7 through 13 are to be answered SOLELY on the basis of the passage below.

Modern management places great emphasis on the concept of communication. The
communication process consists of the steps through which an idea or concept passes from
its inception by one person, the sender, until it is acted upon by another person, the receiver.
Through an understanding of these steps and some of the possible barriers that may occur,
more effective communication may be achieved. The first step in the communication process is
ideation by the sender. This is the formation of the intended content of the message he wants
to transmit. In the next step, encoding, the sender organizes his ideas into a series of symbols designed to communicate his message to his intended receiver. He selects suitable
words or phrases that can be understood by the receiver, and he also selects the appropriate
media to be used—for example, memorandum, conference, etc. The third step is transmission
of the encoded message through selected channels in the organizational structure. In the
fourth step, the receiver enters the process by tuning in to receive the message. If the
receiver does not function, however, the message is lost. For example, if the message is oral,
the receiver must be a good listener. The fifth step is decoding of the message by the
receiver, as for example, by changing words into ideas. At this step, the decoded message
may not be the same idea that the sender originally encoded because the sender and
receiver have different perceptions regarding the meaning of certain words. Finally, the
receiver acts or responds. He may file the information, ask for more information, or take other
action. There can be no assurance, however, that communication has taken place unless
there is some type of feedback to the sender in the form of an acknowledgement that the
message was received.

7. According to the above passage, *ideation* is the process by which the   7.____

   A. sender develops the intended content of the message
   B. sender organizes his ideas into a series of symbols
   C. receiver tunes in to receive the message
   D. receiver decodes the message

8. In the last sentence of the passage, the word *feedback* refers to the process by which the sender is assured that the   8.____

   A. receiver filed the information
   B. receiver's perception is the same as his own
   C. message was received
   D. message was properly interpreted

9. Which one of the following BEST shows the order of the steps in the communication process as described in the passage?   9.____

   A. 1 - ideation   2 - encoding
        3 - decoding   4 - transmission
        5 - receiving   6 - action
        7 - feedback to the sender

   B. 1 - ideation   2 - encoding
        3 - transmission   4 - decoding
        5 - receiving   6 - action
        7 - feedback to the sender

   C. 1 - ideation   2 - decoding
        3 - transmission   4 - receiving
        5 - encoding   6 - action
        7 - feedback to the   sender

   D. 1 - ideation   2 - encoding
        3 - transmission   4 - receiving
        5 - decoding   6 - action
        7 - feedback to the sender

10. Which one of the following BEST expresses the main theme of the passage?   10.____

   A. Different individuals have the same perceptions regarding the meaning of words.
   B. An understanding of the steps in the communication process may achieve better communication.
   C. Receivers play a passive role in the communication process.
   D. Senders should not communicate with receivers who transmit feedback.

11. The above passage implies that a receiver does NOT function properly when he   11.____

   A. transmits feedback   B. files the information
   C. is a poor listener   D. asks for more information

12. Which one of the following, according to the above passage, is included in the SECOND step of the communication process?   12.____

   A. Selecting the appropriate media to be used in transmission
   B. Formulation of the intended content of the message
   C. Using appropriate media to respond to the receiver's feedback
   D. Transmitting the message through selected channels in the organization

13. The above passage implies that the *decoding process* is MOST NEARLY the reverse of the _____ process.   13.____

   A. transmission   B. receiving
   C. feedback   D. encoding

Questions 14-19.

DIRECTIONS: Questions 14 through 19 are to be answered SOLELY on the basis of the following passage.

It is often said that no system will work if the people who carry it out do not want it to work. In too many cases, a departmental reorganization that seemed technically sound and economically practical has proved to be a failure because the planners neglected to take the human factor into account. The truth is that employees are likely to feel threatened when they learn that a major change is in the wind. It does not matter whether or not the change actually poses a threat to an employee; the fact that he believes it does or fears it might is enough to make him feel insecure. Among the dangers he fears, the foremost is the possibility that his job may cease to exist and that he may be laid off or shunted into a less skilled position at lower pay. Even if he knows that his own job category is secure, however, he is likely to fear losing some of the important intangible advantages of his present position—for instance, he may fear that he will be separated from his present companions and thrust in with a group of strangers, or that he will find himself in a lower position on the organizational ladder if a new position is created above his.

It is important that management recognize these natural fears and take them into account in planning any kind of major change. While there is no cut-and-dried formula for preventing employee resistance, there are several steps that can be taken to reduce employees' fears and gain their cooperation. First, unwarranted fears can be dispelled if employees are kept informed of the planning from the start and if they know exactly what to expect. Next, assurance on matters such as retraining, transfers, and placement help should be given as soon as it is clear what direction the reorganization will take. Finally, employees' participation in the planning should be actively sought. There is a great psychological difference between feeling that a change is being forced upon one from the outside, and feeling that one is an insider who is helping to bring about a change.

14. According to the above passage, employees who are not in real danger of losing their jobs because of a proposed reorganization

    A. will be eager to assist in the reorganization
    B. will pay little attention to the reorganization
    C. should not be taken into account in planning the reorganization
    D. are nonetheless likely to feel threatened by the reorganization

14.____

15. The passage mentions the *intangible advantages* of a position.
Which of the following BEST describes the kind of advantages alluded to in the passage?

    A. Benefits such as paid holidays and vacations
    B. Satisfaction of human needs for things like friendship and status
    C. Qualities such as leadership and responsibility
    D. A work environment that meets satisfactory standards of health and safety

15.____

16. According to the passage, an employee's fear that a reorganization may separate him from his present companions is a (n)

    A. childish and immature reaction to change
    B. unrealistic feeling since this is not going to happen

16.____

C. possible reaction that the planners should be aware of
D. incentive to employees to participate in the planning

17. On the basis of the above passage, it would be DESIRABLE, when planning a depart-   17._____
mental reorganization, to

    A. be governed by employee feelings and attitudes
    B. give some employees lower positions
    C. keep employees informed
    D. lay off those who are less skilled

18. What does the passage say can be done to help gain employees' cooperation in a reor-   18._____
ganization?

    A. Making sure that the change is technically sound, that it is economically practical,
       and that the human factor is taken into account
    B. Keeping employees fully informed, offering help in fitting them into new positions,
       and seeking their participation in the planning
    C. Assuring employees that they will not be laid off, that they will not be reassigned to
       a group of strangers, and that no new positions will be created on the organization
       ladder
    D. Reducing employees' fears, arranging a retraining program, and providing for
       transfers

19. Which of the following suggested titles would be MOST appropriate for this passage?   19._____

    A. PLANNING A DEPARTMENTAL REORGANIZATION
    B. WHY EMPLOYEES ARE AFRAID
    C. LOOKING AHEAD TO THE FUTURE
    D. PLANNING FOR CHANGE: THE HUMAN FACTOR

Questions 20-22.

DIRECTIONS: Questions 20 through 22 are to be answered SOLELY on the basis of the fol-
               lowing passage.

    The achievement of good human relations is essential if a business office is to produce
at top efficiency and is to be a pleasant place in which to work. All office workers plan an
important role in handling problems in human relations. They should, therefore, strive to
acquire the understanding, tactfulness, and awareness necessary to deal effectively with
actual office situations involving co-workers on all levels. Only in this way can they truly
become responsible, interested, cooperative, and helpful members of the staff.

20. The selection implies that the MOST important value of good human relations in an office   20._____
is to develop

    A. efficiency   B. cooperativeness
    C. tact   D. pleasantness and efficiency

21. Office workers should acquire understanding in dealing with   21._____

    A. co-workers   B. subordinates
    C. superiors   D. all members of the staff

22. The selection indicates that a highly competent secretary who is also very argumentative   22.____
is meeting office requirements

    A. wholly   B. partly
    C. slightly   D. not at all

Questions 23-25.

DIRECTIONS: Questions 23 through 25 are to be answered SOLELY on the basis of the following passage.

It is common knowledge that ability to do a particular job and performance on the job do
not always go hand in hand. Persons with great potential abilities sometimes fall down on the
job because of laziness or lack of interest in the job, while persons with mediocre talents have
often achieved excellent results through their industry and their loyalty to the interests of their
employers. It is clear; therefore, that in a balanced personnel program, measures of
employee ability need to be supplemented by measures of employee performance, for the
final test of any employee is his performance on the job.

23. The MOST accurate of the following statements, on the basis of the above paragraph, is   23.____
that

    A. employees who lack ability are usually not industrious
    B. an employee's attitudes are more important than his abilities
    C. mediocre employees who are interested in their work are preferable to employees
        who possess great ability
    D. superior capacity for performance should be supplemented with proper attitudes

24. On the basis of the above paragraph, the employee of most value to his employer is NOT   24.____
necessarily the one who

    A. best understands the significance of his duties
    B. achieves excellent results
    C. possesses the greatest talents
    D. produces the greatest amount of work

25. According to the above paragraph, an employee's efficiency is BEST determined by an   25.____

    A. appraisal of his interest in his work
    B. evaluation of the work performed by him
    C. appraisal of his loyalty to his employer
    D. evaluation of his potential ability to perform his work

KEY (CORRECT ANSWERS)

1. B	11. C
2. A	12. A
3. C	13. D
4. C	14. D
5. A	15. B
6. D	16. C
7. A	17. C
8. C	18. B
9. D	19. D
10. B	20. D

21. D
22. B
23. D
24. C
25. B

———

TEST 3

DIRECTIONS: Questions 1 through 8 are to be answered SOLELY on the basis of the following information and directions.

Assume that you are a clerk in a city agency. Your supervisor has asked you to classify each of the accidents that happened to employees in the agency into the following five categories:

A. An accident that occurred in the period from January through June, between 9 A.M. and 12 Noon, that was the result of carelessness on the part of the injured employee, that caused the employee to lose less than seven working hours, that happened to an employee who was 40 years of age or over, and who was employed in the agency for less than three years;

B. An accident that occurred in the period from July through December, after 1 P.M., that was the result of unsafe conditions, that caused the injured employee to lose less than seven working hours, that happened to an employee who was 40 years of age or over, and who was employed in the agency for three years or more;

C. An accident that occurred in the period from January through June, after 1 P.M., that was the result of carelessness on the part of the injured employee, that caused the injured employee to lose seven or more working hours, that happened to an employee who was less than 40 years old, and who was employed in the agency for three years or more;

D. An accident that occurred in the period from July through December, between 9 A.M. and 12 Noon, that was the result of unsafe conditions, that caused the injured employee to lose seven or more working hours, that happened to an employee who was less than 40 years old, and who was employed in the agency for less than three years;

E. Accidents that cannot be classified in any of the foregoing groups. NOTE: In classifying these accidents, an employee's age and length of service are computed as of the date of accident. In all cases, it is to be assumed that each employee has been employed continuously in city service, and that each employee works seven hours a day, from 9 A.M. to 5 P.M., with lunch from 12 Noon to 1 P.M. In each question, consider only the information which will assist you in classifying the accident. Any information which is of no assistance in classifying an accident should not be considered.

1. The unsafe condition of the stairs in the building caused Miss Perkins to have an accident on October 14, 2003 at 4 P.M. When she returned to work the following day at 1 P.M., Miss Perkins said that the accident was the first one that had occurred to her in her ten years of employment with the agency. She was born on April 27, 1962.   1.____

2. On the day after she completed her six-month probationary period of employment with the agency, Miss Green, who had been considered a careful worker by her supervisor, injured her left foot in an accident caused by her own carelessness. She went home immediately after the accident, which occurred at 10 A.M., March 19, 2004, but returned to work at the regular time on the following morning. Miss Green was born July 12, 1963 in New York City.   2.____

3. The unsafe condition of a duplicating machine caused Mr. Martin to injure himself in an accident on September 8, 2006 at 2 P.M. As a result of the accident, he was unable to work the remainder of the day, but returned to his office ready for work on the following morning. Mr. Martin, who has been working for the agency since April 1, 2003, was born in St. Louis on February 1, 1968.

3.____

4. Mr. Smith was hospitalized for two weeks because of a back injury resulted from an accident on the morning of November 16, 2006. Investigation of the accident revealed that it was caused by the unsafe condition of the floor on which Mr. Smith had been walking. Mr. Smith, who is an accountant, has been anemployee of the agency since March 1, 2004, and was born in Ohio on June 10, 1968.

4.____

5. Mr. Allen cut his right hand because he was careless in operating a multilith machine. Mr. Allen, who was 33 years old when the accident took place, has been employed by the agency since August 17, 1992. The accident, which occurred on January 26, 2006, at 2 P.M., caused Mr. Allen to be absent from work for the rest of the day. He was able to return to work the next morning.

5.____

6. Mr. Rand, who is a college graduate, was born on December, 28, 1967, and has been working for the agency since January 7, 2002. On Monday, April 25, 2005, at 2 P.M., his carelessness in operating a duplicating machine caused him to have an accident and to be sent home from work immediately. Fortunately, he was able to return to work at his regular time on the following Wednesday.

6.____

7. Because he was careless in running down a flight of stairs, Mr. Brown fell, bruising his right hand. Although the accident occurred shortly after he arrived for work on the morning of May 22, 2006, he was unable to resume work until 3 P.M. that day. Mr. Brown was born on August 15, 1955, and began working for the agency on September 12, 2003, as a clerk, at a salary of $22,750 per annum.

7.____

8. On December 5, 2005, four weeks after he had begun working for the agency, the unsafe condition of an automatic stapling machine caused Mr. Thomas to injure himself in an accident. Mr. Thomas, who was born on May 19,1975, lost three working days because of the accident, which occurred at 11:45 A.M.

8.____

Questions 9-10.

DIRECTIONS: Questions 9 and 10 are to be answered SOLELY on the basis of the following paragraph.

An impending reorganization within an agency will mean loss by transfer of several professional staff members from the personnel division. The division chief is asked to designate the persons to be transferred. After reviewing the implications of this reduction of staff with his assistant, the division chief discusses the matter at a staff meeting. He adopts the recommendations of several staff members to have volunteers make up the required reduction.

9. The decision to permit personnel to volunteer for transfer is 9.____

    A. *poor,* it is not likely that the members of a division are of equal value to the division chief

    B. *good;* dissatisfied members will probably be more productive elsewhere

    C. *poor;* the division chief has abdicated his responsibility to carry out the order given to him

    D. *good;* morale among remaining staff is likely to improve in a more cohesive framework

10. Suppose that one of the volunteers is a recently appointed employee who has completed his probationary period acceptably, but whose attitude toward division operations and agency administration tends to be rather negative and sometimes even abrasive. Because of his lack of commitment to the division, his transfer is recommended. If the transfer is approved, the division chief should, prior to the transfer, 10.____

    A. discuss with the staff the importance of commitment to the work of the agency and its relationship with job satisfaction

    B. refrain from any discussion of attitude with the employee

    C. discuss with the employee his concern about the employee's attitude

    D. avoid mention of attitude in the evaluation appraisal prepared for the receiving division chief

Questions 11-16.

DIRECTIONS: Questions 11 through 16 are to be answered SOLELY on the basis of the following paragraph.

    Methods of administration of office activities, much of which consists of providing information and *know-how* needed to coordinate both activities within that particular office and other offices, have been among the last to come under the spotlight of management analysis. Progress has been rapid during the past decade, however, and is now accelerating at such a pace that an *information revolution* in office management appears to be in the making. Although triggered by technological breakthroughs in electronic computers and other giant steps in mechanization, this information revolution must be attributed to underlying forces, such as the increased complexity of both governmental and private enterprise, and ever-keener competition. Size, diversification, specialization of function, and decentralization are among the forces which make coordination of activities both more imperative and more difficult. Increased competition, both domestic and international, leaves little margin for error in managerial decisions. Several developments during recent years indicate an evolving pattern. In 1960, the American Management Association expanded the scope of its activities and changed the name of its Office Management Division to Administrative Services Division. Also in 1960, the magazine *Office Management* merged with the magazine *American Business,* and this new publication was named *Administrative Management.*

11. A REASONABLE inference that can be made from the information in the above paragraph is that an important role of the office manager today is to

    A. work toward specialization of functions performed by his subordinates
    B. inform and train subordinates regarding any new developments in computer technology and mechanization
    C. assist the professional management analysts with the management analysis work in the organization
    D. supply information that can be used to help coordinate and manage the other activities of the organization

11.____

12. An IMPORTANT reason for the *information revolution* that has been taking place in office management is the

    A. advance made in management analysis in the past decade
    B. technological breakthrough in electronic computers and mechanization
    C. more competitive and complicated nature of private business and government
    D. increased efficiency of office management techniques in the past ten years

12.____

13. According to the above paragraph, specialization of function in an organization is MOST likely to result in

    A. the elimination of errors in managerial decisions
    B. greater need to coordinate activities
    C. more competition with other organizations, both domestic and international
    D. a need for office managers with greater flexibility

13.____

14. The word *evolving,* as used in the third from last sentence in the above paragraph, means MOST NEARLY

    A. developing by gradual changes
    B. passing on to others
    C. occurring periodically
    D. breaking up into separate, constituent parts

14.____

15. Of the following, the MOST reasonable implication of the changes in names mentioned in the last part of the above paragraph is that these groups are attempting to

    A. professionalize the field of office management and the title of Office Manager
    B. combine two publications into one because of the increased costs of labor and materials
    C. adjust to the fact that the field of office management is broadening
    D. appeal to the top managerial people rather than the office management people in business and government

15.____

16. According to the above paragraph, intense competition among domestic and international enterprises makes it MOST important for an organization's managerial staff to

    A. coordinate and administer office activities with other activities in the organization
    B. make as few errors in decision-making as possible
    C. concentrate on decentralization and reduction of size of the individual divisions of the organization
    D. restrict decision-making only to top management officials

16.____

Questions 17-21.

DIRECTIONS: Questions 17 through 21 are to be answered SOLELY on the basis of the following passage.

For some office workers, it is useful to be familiar with the four main classes of domestic
mail; for others, it is essential. Each class has a different rate of postage, and some have
requirements concerning wrapping, sealing, or special information to be placed on the package. First class mail, the class which may not be opened for postal inspection, includes letters, postcards, business reply cards, and other kinds of written matter. There are different
rates for some of the kinds of cards which can be sent by first class mail. The maximum
weight for an item sent by first class mail is 70 pounds. An item which is not letter size should
be marked *First Class* on all sides. Although office workers most often come into contact with
first class mail, they may find it helpful to know something about the other classes. Second
class mail is generally used for mailing newspapers and magazines. Publishers of these articles must meet certain U.S. Postal Service requirements in order to obtain a permit to use
second class mailing rates. Third class mail, which must weigh less than 1 pound, includes
printed materials and merchandise parcels. There are two rate structures for this class - a
single piece rate and a bulk rate. Fourth class mail, also known as parcel post, includes packages weighing from one to 40 pounds. For more information about these classes of mail and
the actual mailing rates, contact your local post office.

17.   According to this passage, first class mail is the *only* class which   17._____

    A.   has a limit on the maximum weight of an item
    B.   has different rates for items within the class
    C.   may not be opened for postal inspection
    D.   should be used by office workers

18.   According to this passage, the one of the following items which may CORRECTLY be   18._____
sent by fourth class mail is a

    A.   magazine weighing one-half pound
    B.   package weighing one-half pound
    C.   package weighing two pounds
    D.   postcard

19.   According to this passage, there are different postage rates for   19._____

    A.   a newspaper sent by second class mail and a magazine sent by second class mail
    B.   each of the classes of mail
    C.   each pound of fourth class mail
    D.   printed material sent by third class mail and merchandise parcels sent by third
         class mail

20.   In order to send a newspaper by second class mail, a publisher MUST   20._____

    A.   have met certain postal requirements and obtained a permit
    B.   indicate whether he wants to use the single piece or the bulk rate
    C.   make certain that the newspaper weighs less than one pound
    D.   mark the newspaper *Second Class* on the top and bottom of the wrapper

21. Of the following types of information, the one which is NOT mentioned in the passage is   21.____
    the

    A. class of mail to which parcel post belongs
    B. kinds of items which can be sent by each class of mail
    C. maximum weight for an item sent by fourth class mail
    D. postage rate for each of the four classes of mail

Questions 22-25.

DIRECTIONS: Questions 22 through 25 are to be answered SOLELY on the basis of the fol-
              lowing paragraph.

A standard comprises characteristics attached to an aspect of a process or product by
which it can be evaluated. Standardization is the development and adoption of standards.
When they are formulated, standards are not usually the product of a single person, but represent the thoughts and ideas of a group, leavened with the knowledge and information which
are currently available. Standards which do not meet certain basic requirements become a
hindrance rather than an aid to progress. Standards must not only be correct, accurate, and
precise in requiring no more and no less than what is needed for satisfactory results, but they
must also be workable in the sense that their usefulness is not nullified by external conditions.
Standards should also be acceptable to the people who use them. If they are not acceptable,
they cannot be considered to be satisfactory, although they may possess all the other essential characteristics.

22. According to the above paragraph, a processing standard that requires the use of mate-   22.____
    rials that cannot be procured is MOST likely to be

    A. incomplete   B. unworkable
    C. inaccurate   D. unacceptable

23. According to the above paragraph, the construction of standards to which the perfor-   23.____
    mance of job duties should conform is MOST often

    A. the work of the people responsible for seeing that the duties are properly per-
       formed
    B. accomplished by the person who is best informed about the functions involved
    C. the responsibility of the people who are to apply them
    D. attributable to the efforts of various informed persons

24. According to the above paragraph, when standards call for finer tolerances than those   24.____
    essential to the conduct of successful production operations, the effect of the standards
    on the improvement of production operations is

    A. negative   B. negligible
    C. nullified   D. beneficial

25. The one of the following which is the MOST suitable title for the above paragraph is   25.____

    A. THE EVALUATION OF FORMULATED STANDARDS
    B. THE ATTRIBUTES OF SATISFACTORY STANDARDS
    C. THE ADOPTION OF ACCEPTABLE STANDARDS
    D. THE USE OF PROCESS OR PRODUCT STANDARDS

KEY (CORRECT ANSWERS)

1.	B	11.	D
2.	A	12.	C
3.	E	13.	B
4.	D	14.	A
5.	E	15.	C
6.	C	16.	B
7.	A	17.	C
8.	D	18.	C
9.	A	19.	B
10.	C	20.	A

21.	D
22.	C
23.	D
24.	A
25.	B

RECORD KEEPING
EXAMINATION SECTION
TEST 1

DIRECTIONS: Each question or incomplete statement is followed by several suggested answers or completions. Select the one that BEST answers the question or completes the statement. *PRINT THE LETTER OF THE CORRECT ANSWER IN THE SPACE AT THE RIGHT.*

Questions 1-7.

DIRECTIONS: In answering Questions 1 through 7, use the following master list. For each question, determine where the name would fit on the master list. Each answer choice indicates right before or after the name in the answer choice.

Aaron, Jane
Armstead, Brendan
Bailey, Charles
Dent, Ricardo
Grant, Mark
Mars, Justin
Methieu, Justine
Parker, Cathy
Sampson, Suzy
Thomas, Heather

1. Schmidt, William
   A. Right before Cathy Parker
   B. Right after Heather Thomas
   C. Right after Suzy Sampson
   D. Right before Ricardo Dent

1.____

2. Asanti, Kendall
   A. Right before Jane Aaron
   B. Right after Charles Bailey
   C. Right before Justine Methieu
   D. Right after Brendan Armstead

2.____

3. O'Brien, Daniel
   A. Right after Justine Methieu
   B. Right before Jane Aaron
   C. Right after Mark Grant
   D. Right before Suzy Sampson

3.____

4. Marrow, Alison
   A. Right before Cathy Parker
   B. Right before Justin Mars
   C. Right after Mark Grant
   D. Right after Heather Thomas

4.____

5. Grantt, Marissa
   A. Right before Mark Grant
   B. Right after Mark Grant
   C. Right after Justin Mars
   D. Right before Suzy Sampson

5.____

6. Thompson, Heath   6.____
   A. Right after Justin Mars   B. Right before Suzy Sampson
   C. Right after Heather Thomas   D. Right before Cathy Parker

DIRECTIONS: Before answering Question 7, add in all of the names from Questions 1 through
             6. Then fit the name in alphabetical order based on the new list.

7. Francisco, Mildred   7.____
   A. Right before Mark Grant   B. Right after Marissa Grantt
   C. Right before Alison Marrow   D. Right after Kendall Asanti

Questions 8-10.

DIRECTIONS: In answering Questions 8 through 10, compare each pair of names and
             addresses. Indicate whether they are the same or different in any way.

8. William H. Pratt, J.D.   William H. Pratt, J.D.   8.____
   Attourney at Law   Attorney at Law
   A. No differences   B. 1 difference
   C. 2 differences   D. 3 differences

9. 1303 Theater Drive,; Apt. 3-B   1330 Theatre Drive,; Apt. 3-B 9.____
   A. No differences   B. 1 difference
   C. 2 differences   D. 3 differences

10. Petersdorff, Briana and Mary   Petersdorff, Briana and Mary 10.____
    A. No differences   B. 1 difference
    C. 2 differences   D. 3 differences

11. Which of the following words, if any, are misspelled?   11.____
    A. Affordable   B. Circumstansial
    C. Legalese   D. None of the above

Questions 12-13.

DIRECTIONS: Questions 12 and 13 are to be answered on the basis of the following table.

Standardized Test Results for High School Students in District #1230

	English	Math	Science	Reading
High School 1	21	22	15	18
High School 2	12	16	13	15
High School 3	16	18	21	17
High School 4	19	14	15	16

The scores for each high school in the district were averaged out and listed for each subject tested. Scores of 0-10 are significantly below College Readiness Standards. 11-15 are below College Readiness, 16-20 meet College Readiness, and 21-25 are above College Readiness.

12. If the high schools need to meet or exceed in at least half the categories   12._____
    in order to NOT be considered "at risk," which schools are considered "at risk"?
    A. High School 2   B. High School 3
    C. High School 4   D. Both A and C

13. What percentage of subjects did the district as a whole meet or exceed   13._____
    College Readiness standards?
    A. 25%   B. 50%   C. 75%   D. 100%

Questions 14-15.

DIRECTIONS: Questions 14 and 15 are to be answered on the basis of the following
              information.

You have seven employees working as a part of your team: Austin, Emily, Jeremy,
Christina, Martin, Harriet, and Steve. You have just sent an e-mail informing them that
there will be a mandatory training session next week. To ensure that work still gets done,
you are offering the training twice during the week: once on Tuesday and also on
Thursday. This way half the employees will still be working while the other half attend the
training. The only other issue is that Jeremy doesn't work on Tuesdays and Harriet
doesn't work on Thursdays due to compressed work schedules.

14. Which of the following is a possible attendance roster for the first training   14._____
    session?
    A. Emily, Jeremy, Steve   B. Steve, Christina, Harriet
    C. Harriet, Jeremy, Austin   D. Steve, Martin, Jeremy

15. If Harriet, Christina, and Steve attend the training session on Tuesday, which   15._____
    of the following is a possible roster for Thursday's training session?
    A. Jeremy, Emily, and Austin   B. Emily, Martin, and Harriet
    C. Austin, Christina, and Emily   D. Jeremy, Emily, and Steve

Questions 16-20.

DIRECTIONS: In answering Questions 16 through 20, you will be given a word and will need
              to choose the answer choice that is MOST similar or different to the word.

16. Which word means the SAME as *annual*?   16._____
    A. Monthly   B. Usually   C. Yearly   D. Constantly

17. Which word means the SAME as *effort*?   17._____
    A. Energy   B. Equate   C. Cherish   D. Commence

18. Which word means the OPPOSITE of *forlorn*?   18._____
    A. Neglected   B. Lethargy   C. Optimistic   D. Astonished

19. Which word means the SAME as *risk*?   19._____
    A. Admire   B. Hazard   C. Limit   D. Hesitant

20. Which word means the OPPOSITE of *translucent*?
    A. Opaque   B. Transparent   C. Luminous   D. Introverted

20.____

21. Last year, Jamie's annual salary was $50,000. Her boss called her today to inform her that she would receive a 20% raise for the upcoming year. How much more money will Jamie receive next year?
    A. $60,000   B. $10,000   C. $1,000   D. $51,000

21.____

22. You and a co-worker work for a temp hiring agency as part of their office staff. You both are given 6 days off per month. How many days off are you and your co-worker given in a year?
    A. 24   B. 72   C. 144   D. 48

22.____

23. If Margot makes $34,000 per year and she works 40 hours per week for all 52 weeks, what is her hourly rate?
    A. $16.34/hour   B. $17.00/hour   C. $15.54/hour   D. $13.23/hour

23.____

24. How many dimes are there in $175.00?
    A. 175   B. 1,750   C. 3,500   D. 17,500

24.____

25. If Janey is three times as old as Emily, and Emily is 3, how old is Janey?
    A. 6   B. 9   C. 12   D. 15

25.____

KEY (CORRECT ANSWERS)

1.	C		11.	B
2.	D		12.	A
3.	A		13.	D
4.	B		14.	B
5.	B		15.	A
6.	C		16.	C
7.	A		17.	A
8.	B		18.	C
9.	C		19.	B
10.	A		20.	A

21.	B
22.	C
23.	A
24.	B
25.	B

TEST 2

DIRECTIONS: Each question or incomplete statement is followed by several suggested answers or completions. Select the one that BEST answers the question or completes the statement. *PRINT THE LETTER OF THE CORRECT ANSWER IN THE SPACE AT THE RIGHT.*

Questions 1-6.

DIRECTIONS: Questions 1 through 6 are to be answered on the basis of the following information.

item	name of item to be ordered
quantity	minimum number that can be ordered
beginning amount	amount in stock at start of month
amount received	amount receiving during month
ending amount	amount in stock at end of month
amount used	amount used during month
amount to order	will need at least as much of each item as used in the previous month
unit price	cost of each unit of an item
total price	total price for the order

Item	Quantity	Beginning	Received	Ending	Amount Used	Amount to Order	Unit Price	Total Price
Pens	10	22	10	8	24	20	$0.11	$2.20
Spiral notebooks	8	30	13	12			$0.25	
Binder clips	2 boxes	3 boxes	1 box	1 box			$1.79	
Sticky notes	3 packs	12 packs	4 packs	2 packs			$1.29	
Dry erase markers	1 pack (dozen)	34 markers	8 markers	40 markers			$16.49	
Ink cartridges (printer)	1 cartridge	3 cartridges	1 cartridge	2 cartridges			$79.99	
Folders	10 folders	25 folders	15 folders	10 folders			$1.08	

1. How many packs of sticky notes were used during the month? 1.____
   A. 16   B. 10   C. 12   D. 14

2. How many folders need to be ordered for next month? 2.____
   A. 15   B. 20   C. 30   D. 40

3. What is the total price of notebooks that you will need to order? 3.____
   A. $6.00   B. $0.25   C. $4.50   D. $2.75

4. Which of the following will you spend the second most money on? 4.____
   A. Ink cartridges   B. Dry erase markers
   C. Sticky notes   D. Binder clips

5. How many packs of dry erase markers should you order? 5.____
   A. 1   B. 8   C. 12   D. 0

6. What will be the total price of the file folders you order?   6._____
    A. $20.16   B. $2.16   C. $1.08   D. $4.32

Questions 7-11.

DIRECTIONS: Questions 7 through 11 are to be answered on the basis of the following table.

Number of Car Accidents, By Location and Cause, for 2014						
	Location 1		Location 2		Location 3	
Cause	Number	Percent	Number	Percent	Number	Percent
Severe Weather	10		25		30	
Excessive Speeding	20	40	5		10	
Impaired Driving	15		15	25	8	
Miscellaneous	5		15		2	4
TOTALS	50	100	60	100	50	100

7. Which of the following is the third highest cause of accidents for all three locations?   7._____
    A. Severe Weather   B. Impaired Driving
    C. Miscellaneous   D. Excessive Speeding

8. The average number of Severe Weather accidents per week at Location 3 for the year (52 weeks) was MOST NEARLY   8._____
    A. 0.57   B. 30   C. 1   D. 1.25

9. Which location had the LARGEST percentage of accidents caused by Impaired Driving?   9._____
    A. 1   B. 2   C. 3   D. Both A and B

10. If one-third of the accidents at all three locations resulted in at least one fatality, what is the LEAST amount of deaths caused by accidents last year?   10._____
    A. 60   B. 106   C. 66   D. 53

11. What is the percentage of accidents caused by miscellaneous means from all three locations in 2014?   11._____
    A. 5%   B. 10%   C. 13%   D. 25%

12. How many pairs of the following groups of letters are exactly alike?   12._____

    ACDOBJ   ACDBOJ
    HEWBWR   HEWRWB
    DEERVS   DEERVS
    BRFQSX   BRFQSX
    WEYRVB   WEYRVB
    SPQRZA   SQRPZA

    A. 2   B. 3   C. 4   D. 5

Questions 13-19.

DIRECTIONS: Questions 13 through 19 are to be answered on the basis of the following
            information.

In 2012, the most current information on the American population was finished. The
information was compiled by 200 volunteers in each of the 50 states. The territory of Puerto
Rico, a sovereign of the United States, had 25 people assigned to compile data. In February of
2010, volunteers in each state and sovereign began collecting information. In Puerto Rico, data
collection finished by January 31st, 2011, while work in the United States was completed on
June 30, 2012. Each volunteer gathered data on the population of their state or sovereign.
When the information was compiled, volunteers sent reports to the nation's capital, Washington,
D.C. Each volunteer worked 20 hours per month and put together 10 reports per month. After
the data was compiled in total, 50 people reviewed the data and worked from January 2012 to
December 2012.

13. How many reports were generated from February 2010 to April 2010 in Illinois   13.____
     and Ohio?
         A. 3,000   B. 6,000   C. 12,000   D. 15,000

14. How many volunteers in total collected population data in January 2012?   14.____
         A. 10,000   B. 2,000   C. 225   D. 200

15. How many reports were put together in May 2012?   15.____
         A. 2,000   B. 50,000   C. 100,000   D. 100,250

16. How many hours did the Puerto Rican volunteers work in the fall   16.____
     (September-November)?
         A. 60   B. 500   C. 1,500   D. 0

17. How many workers were compiling or reviewing data in July 2012?   17.____
         A. 25   B. 50   C. 200   D. 250

18. What was the total amount of hours worked by Nevada volunteers in July 2010?   18.____
         A. 500   B. 4,000   C. 4,500   D. 5,000

19. How many reviewers worked in January 2013?   19.____
         A. 75   B. 50   C. 0   D. 25

20. John has to file 10 documents per shelf. How many documents would it   20.____
     take for John to fill 40 shelves?
         A. 40   B. 400   C. 4,500   D. 5,000

21. Jill wants to travel from New York City to Los Angeles by bike, which   21.____
     is approximately 2,772 miles. How many miles per day would Jill need to
     average if she wanted to complete the trip in 4 weeks?
         A. 100   B. 89   C. 99   D. 94

22. If there are 24 CPU's and only 7 monitors, how many more monitors do you need to have the same amount of monitors as CPU's?

    A. Not enough information   B. 17

    C. 31   D. 0

22.____

23. If Gerry works 5 days a week and 8 hours each day, and John works 3 days a week and 10 hours each day, how many more hours per year will Gerry work than John?

    A. They work the same amount of hours.

    B. 450

    C. 520

    D. 832

23.____

24. Jimmy gets transferred to a new office. The new office has 25 employees, but only 16 are there due to a blizzard. How many coworkers was Jimmy able to meet on his first day?

    A. 16   B. 25   C. 9   D. 7

24.____

25. If you do a fundraiser for charities in your area and raise $500 total, how much would you give to each charity if you were donating equal amounts to 3 of them?

    A. $250.00   B. $167.77   C. $50.00   D. $111.11

25.____

KEY (CORRECT ANSWERS)

1.	D		11.	C
2.	B		12.	B
3.	A		13.	C
4.	C		14.	A
5.	D		15.	C
6.	B		16.	C
7.	D		17.	B
8.	A		18.	B
9.	A		19.	C
10.	D		20.	B

21.	C
22.	B
23.	C
24.	A
25.	B

TEST 3

DIRECTIONS: Each question or incomplete statement is followed by several suggested answers or completions. Select the one that BEST answers the question or completes the statement. *PRINT THE LETTER OF THE CORRECT ANSWER IN THE SPACE AT THE RIGHT.*

Questions 1-3.

DIRECTIONS: In answering Questions 1 through 3, choose the correctly spelled word.

1. A. allusion   B. alusion   C. allusien   D. allution   1._____

2. A. altitude   B. alltitude   C. atlitude   D. altlitude   2._____

3. A. althogh   B. allthough   C. althrough   D. although   3._____

Questions 4-9.

DIRECTIONS: In answering Questions 4 through 9, choose the answer that BEST completes the analogy.

4. Odometer is to mileage as compass is to   4._____
   A. speed   B. needle   C. hiking   D. direction

5. Marathon is to race as hibernation is to   5._____
   A. winter   B. dream   C. sleep   D. bear

6. Cup is to coffee as bowl is to   6._____
   A. dish   B. spoon   C. food   D. soup

7. Flow is to river as stagnant is to   7._____
   A. pool   B. rain   C. stream   D. canal

8. Paw is to cat as hoof is to   8._____
   A. lamb   B. horse   C. lion   D. elephant

9. Architect is to building as sculptor is to   9._____
   A. museum   B. chisel   C. stone   D. statue

Questions 10-14.

DIRECTIONS: Questions 10 through 14 are to be answered on the basis of the following graph.

Population of Carroll City Broken Down by Age and Gender (in Thousands)			
Age	Female	Male	Total
Under 15	60	60	120
15-23		22	
24-33		20	44
34-43	13	18	31
44-53	20		67
64 and Over	65	65	130
TOTAL	230	232	462

10.   How many people in the city are between the ages of 15-23?   10._____
       A. 70   B. 46,000   C. 70,000   D. 225,000

11.   Approximately what percentage of the total population of the city was   11._____
       female aged 24-33?
       A. 10%   B. 5%   C. 15%   D. 25%

12.   If 33% of the males have a job and 55% of females don't have a job,   12._____
       which of the following statements is TRUE?
       A. Males have approximately 2,600 more jobs than females.
       B. Females have approximately 49,000 more jobs than males.
       C. Females have approximately 26,000 more jobs than males.
       D. None of the above statements are true.

13.   How many females between the ages of 15-23 live in Carroll City?   13._____
       A. 67,000   B. 24,000   C. 48,000   D. 91,000

14.   Assume all males 44-53 living in Carroll City are employed. If two-thirds   14._____
       of males age 44-53 work jobs outside of Carroll City, how many work within city
       limits?
       A. 31,333
       B. 15,667
       C. 47,000
       D. Cannot answer the question with the information provided

Questions 15-16.

DIRECTIONS: Questions 15 and 16 are labeled as shown. Alphabetize them for filing.
Choose the answer that correctly shows the order.

15. (1) AED   15.____
    (2) OOS
    (3) FOA
    (4) DOM
    (5) COB

    A. 2-5-4-3-2   B. 1-4-5-2-3   C. 1-5-4-2-3   D. 1-5-4-3-2

16. Alphabetize the names of the people. Last names are given last.   16.____
    (1) Lindsey Jamestown
    (2) Jane Alberta
    (3) Ally Jamestown
    (4) Allison Johnston
    (5) Lyle Moreno

    A. 2-1-3-4-5   B. 3-4-2-1-5   C. 2-3-1-4-5   D. 4-3-2-1-5

17. Which of the following words is misspelled?   17.____
    A. disgust   B. whisper
    C. locale   D. none of the above

Questions 18-21.

DIRECTIONS: Questions 18 through 21 are to be answered on the basis of the following list of
employees.

    Robertson, Aaron
    Bacon, Gina
    Jerimiah, Trace
    Gillette, Stanley
    Jacks, Sharon

18. Which employee name would come in third in alphabetized list?   18.____
    A. Robertson, Aaron   B. Jerimiah, Trace
    C. Gillette, Stanley   D. Jacks, Sharon

19. Which employee's first name starts with the letter in the alphabet that is   19.____
    five letters after the first letter of their last name?
    A. Jerimiah, Trace   B. Bacon, Gina
    C. Jacks, Sharon   D. Gillette, Stanley

20. How many employees have last names that are exactly five letters long?   20.____
    A. 1   B. 2   C. 3   D. 4

21. How many of the employees have either a first or last name that starts with the letter "G"?
    A. 1   B. 2   C. 4   D. 5   21._____

Questions 22-25.

DIRECTIONS: Questions 22 through 25 are to be answered on the basis of the following chart.

Bicycle Sales (Model #34JA32)							
Country	May	June	July	August	September	October	Total
Germany	34	47	45	54	56	60	296
Britain	40	44	36	47	47	46	260
Ireland	37	32	32	32	34	33	200
Portugal	14	14	14	16	17	14	89
Italy	29	29	28	31	29	31	177
Belgium	22	24	24	26	25	23	144
Total	176	198	179	206	208	207	1166

22. What percentage of the overall total was sold to the German importer?   22._____
    A. 25.3%   B. 22%   C. 24.1%   D. 23%

23. What percentage of the overall total was sold in September?   23._____
    A. 24.1%   B. 25.6%   C. 17.9%   D. 24.6%

24. What is the average number of units per month imported into Belgium over the first four months shown?   24._____
    A. 26   B. 20   C. 24   D. 31

25. If you look at the three smallest importers, what is their total import percentage?   25._____
    A. 35.1%   B. 37.1%   C. 40%   D. 28%

KEY (CORRECT ANSWERS)

1.	A		11.	B
2.	A		12.	C
3.	D		13.	C
4.	D		14.	B
5.	C		15.	D
6.	D		16.	C
7.	A		17.	D
8.	B		18.	D
9.	D		19.	B
10.	C		20.	B

21.	B
22.	A
23.	C
24.	C
25.	A

TEST 4

DIRECTIONS: Each question or incomplete statement is followed by several suggested answers or completions. Select the one that BEST answers the question or completes the statement. *PRINT THE LETTER OF THE CORRECT ANSWER IN THE SPACE AT THE RIGHT.*

Questions 1-6.

DIRECTIONS: In answering Questions 1 through 6, choose the sentence that represents the BEST example of English grammar.

1. A. Joey and me want to go on a vacation next week.
   B. Gary told Jim he would need to take some time off.
   C. If turning six years old, Jim's uncle would teach Spanish to him.
   D. Fax a copy of your resume to Ms. Perez and me.

   1._____

2. A. Jerry stood in line for almost two hours.
   B. The reaction to my engagement was less exciting than I thought it would be.
   C. Carlos and me have done great work on this project.
   D. Two parts of the speech needs to be revised before tomorrow.

   2._____

3. A. Arriving home, the alarm was tripped.
   B. Jonny is regarded as a stand up guy, a responsible parent, and he doesn't give up until a task is finished.
   C. Each employee must submit a drug test each month.
   D. One of the documents was incinerated in the explosion.

   3._____

4. A. As soon as my parents get home, I told them I finished all of my chores.
   B. I asked my teacher to send me my missing work, check my absences, and how did I do on my test.
   C. Matt attempted to keep it concealed from Jenny and me.
   D. If Mary or him cannot get work done on time, I will have to split them up.

   4._____

5. A. Driving to work, the traffic report warned him of an accident on Highway 47.
   B. Jimmy has performed well this season.
   C. Since finishing her degree, several job offers have been given to Cam.
   D. Our boss is creating unstable conditions for we employees.

   5._____

6. A. The thief was described as a tall man with a wiry mustache weighing approximately 150 pounds.
   B. She gave Patrick and I some more time to finish our work.
   C. One of the books that he ordered was damaged in shipping.
   D. While talking on the rotary phone, the car Jim was driving skidded off the road.

   6._____

Questions 7-9.

DIRECTIONS: Questions 7 through 9 are to be answered on the basis of the following graph.

Ice Lake Frozen Flight (2002-2013)		
Year	Number of Participants	Temperature (Fahrenheit)
2002	22	4°
2003	50	33°
2004	69	18°
2005	104	22°
2006	108	24°
2007	288	33°
2008	173	9°
2009	598	39°
2010	698	26°
2011	696	30°
2012	777	28°
2013	578	32°

7. Which two year span had the LARGEST difference between temperatures?   7._____
   A. 2002 and 2003   B. 2011 and 2012
   C. 2008 and 2009   D. 2003 and 2004

8. How many total people participated in the years after the temperature   8._____
   reached at least 29°?
   A. 2,295   B. 1,717   C. 2,210   D. 4,543

9. In 2007, the event saw 288 participants, while in 2008 that number   9._____
   dropped to 173. Which of the following reasons BEST explains the drop in
   participants?
   A. The event had not been going on that long and people didn't know about
      it.
   B. The lake water wasn't cold enough to have people jump in.
   C. The temperature was too cold for many people who would have normally
      participated.
   D. None of the above reasons explain the drop in participants.

10. In the following list of numbers, how many times does 4 come just after 2   10._____
    when 2 comes just after an odd number?
    23652476538986324885724863924242
    A. 2   B. 3   C. 4   D. 5

11. Which choice below lists the letter that is as far after B as S is after N in   11._____
    the alphabet?
    A. G   B. H   C. I   D. J

Questions 12-15.

DIRECTIONS: Questions 12 through 15 are to be answered on the basis of the following directory and list of changes.

Directory		
Name	Emp. Type	Position
Julie Taylor	Warehouse	Packer
James King	Office	Administrative Assistant
John Williams	Office	Salesperson
Ray Moore	Warehouse	Maintenance
Kathleen Byrne	Warehouse	Supervisor
Amy Jones	Office	Salesperson
Paul Jonas	Office	Salesperson
Lisa Wong	Warehouse	Loader
Eugene Lee	Office	Accountant
Bruce Lavine	Office	Manager
Adam Gates	Warehouse	Packer
Will Suter	Warehouse	Packer
Gary Lorper	Office	Accountant
Jon Adams	Office	Salesperson
Susannah Harper	Office	Salesperson

Directory Updates:
- Employee e-mail address will adhere to the following guidelines: lastnamefirstname@apexindustries.com (ex. Susannah Harper is harpersusannah@apexindustries.com). Currently, employees in the warehouse share one e-mail, distribution@apexindustries.com.
- The "Loader" position was now be referred to as "Specialist I"
- Adam Gates has accepted a Supervisor position within the Warehouse and is no longer a Packer. All warehouses employees report to the two Supervisors and all office employees report to the Manager.

12.   Amy Jones tried to send an e-mail to Adam Gates, but it wouldn't send.   12.____
      Which of the following offers the BEST explanation?
      A. Amy put Adam's first name first and then his last name.
      B. Adam doesn't check his e-mail, so he wouldn't know if he received the e-mail or not.
      C. Adam does not have his own e-mail.
      D. Office employees are not allowed to send e-mails to each other.

13.   How many Packers currently work for Apex Industries?   13.____
      A. 2   B. 3   C. 4   D. 5

14.   What position does Lisa Wong currently hold?   14.____
      A. Specialist I   B. Secretary
      C. Administrative Assistant   D. Loader

15. If an employee wanted to contact the office manager, which of the following e-mails should the e-mail be sent to?
    A. officemanager@apexindustries.com
    B. brucelavine@apexindustries.com
    C. lavinebruce@apexindustries.com
    D. distribution@apexindustries.com

15.____

Questions 16-19.

DIRECTIONS: In answering Questions 16 through 19, compare the three names, numbers or addresses.

16. Smiley Yarnell   Smiley Yarnel   Smily Yarnell   16.____
    A. All three are exactly alike.
    B. The first and second are exactly alike.
    C. The second and third are exactly alike.
    D. All three are different.

17. 1583 Theater Drive   1583 Theater Drive   1583 Theatre Drive   17.____
    A. All three are exactly alike.
    B. The first and second are exactly alike.
    C. The second and third are exactly alike.
    D. All three are different.

18. 3341893212   3341893212   3341893212   18.____
    A. All three are exactly alike.
    B. The first and second are exactly alike.
    C. The second and third are exactly alike.
    D. All three are different.

19. Douglass Watkins   Douglas Watkins   Douglass Watkins   19.____
    A. All three are exactly alike.
    B. The first and third are exactly alike.
    C. The second and third are exactly alike.
    D. All three are different.

Questions 20-24.

DIRECTIONS: In answering Questions 20 through 24, you will be presented with a word. Choose the synonym that BEST represents the word in question.

20. Flexible   20.____
    A. delicate   B. inflammable   C. strong   D. pliable

21. Alternative   21.____
    A. choice   B. moderate   C. lazy   D. value

22. Corroborate
    A. examine   B. explain   C. verify   D. explain   22.____

23. Respiration
    A. recovery   B. breathing   C. sweating   D. selfish   23.____

24. Negligent
    A. lazy   B. moderate   C. hopeless   D. lax   24.____

25. Plumber is to Wrench as Painter is to
    A. pipe   B. shop   C. hammer   D. brush   25.____

KEY (CORRECT ANSWERS)

1.	D		11.	A
2.	A		12.	C
3.	D		13.	A
4.	C		14.	A
5.	B		15.	C
6.	C		16.	D
7.	C		17.	B
8.	B		18.	A
9.	C		19.	B
10.	C		20.	D

21. A
22. C
23. B
24. D
25. D

FILING

EXAMINATION SECTION
TEST 1

DIRECTIONS: Questions 1 through 8 each show in Column I names written on four cards (lettered w, x, y, z) which have to be filed. You are to choose the option (lettered A, B, C, or D) in Column II which *BEST* represents the proper order of filing according to the Rules for Alphabetic Filing, given before, and the sample question given below. Print the letter of the correct answer in the space at the right.

SAMPLE QUESTION

	Column I		Column II
w.	Jane Earl	A.	w, y, z, x
x.	James A. Earle	B.	y, w, z, x
y.	James Earl	C.	x, y, w, z
z.	J. Earle	D.	x, w, y, z

The correct way to file the cards is:
y.	James Earl
w.	Jane Earl
z.	J. Earle
x.	James A. Earle

The correct filing order is shown by the letters, y, w, z, x (in that sequence). Since, in Column II, B appears in front of the letters, y, w, z, x (in that sequence), B is the correct answer to the sample question.

Now answer the following questions using that same procedure.

		Column I		Column II	
1.	w.	James Rothschild	A.	x, z, w, y	1.____
	x.	Julius B. Rothchild	B.	x, w, z, y	
	y.	B. Rothstein	C.	z, y, w, x	
	z.	Brian Joel Rothenstein	D.	z, w, x, y	
2.	w.	George S. Wise	A.	w, y, z, x	2.____
	x.	S. G. Wise	B.	x, w, y, z	
	y.	Geo. Stuart Wise	C.	y, x, w, z	
	z.	Prof. Diana Wise	D.	z, w, y, x	
3.	w.	10th Street Bus Terminal	A.	x, z, w, y	3.____
	x.	Buckingham Travel Agency	B.	y, x, w, z	
	y.	The Buckingham Theater	C.	w, z, y, x	
	z.	Burt Tompkins Studio	D.	x, w, y, z	
4.	w.	National Council of American Importers	A.	w, y, x, z	4.____
			B.	x, z, w, y	
	x.	National Chain Co. of Providence	C.	z, x, w, y	
	y.	National Council on Alcoholism	D.	z, x, y, w	
	z.	National Chain Co.			

5.   w.   Dr. Herbert Alvary   A.   w, y, x, z   5.____
      x.   Mr. Victor Alvarado   B.   z, w, x, y
      y.   Alvar Industries   C.   y, z, x, w
      z.   V. Alvarado   D.   w, z, x, y

6.   w.   Joan MacBride   A.   w, x, z, y   6.____
      x.   Wm. Mackey   B.   w, y, z, x
      y.   Roslyn McKenzie   C.   w, z, x, y
      z.   Winifred Mackey   D.   w, y, x, z

7.   w.   3 Way Trucking Co.   A.   y, x, z, w   7.____
      x.   3rd Street Bakery   B.   y, z, w, x
      y.   380 Realty Corp.   C.   x, y, z, w
      z.   Three Lions Pub   D.   x, y, w, z

8.   w.   Miss Rose Leonard   A.   z, w, x, y   8.____
      x.   Rev. Leonard Lucas   B.   w, z, y, x
      y.   Sylvia Leonard Linen Shop   C.   w, x, z, y
      z.   Rose S. Leonard   D.   z, w, y, x

KEY (CORRECT ANSWERS)

1.   A
2.   D
3.   B
4.   D
5.   C
6.   A
7.   C
8.   B

TEST 2

DIRECTIONS: Questions 1 through 7 each show in Column I four names (lettered w, x, y, z) which have to be entered in an agency telephone directory. You are to choose the option (lettered A, B, C, or D) in Column II which *BEST* represents the proper order for entering them according to the Rules for Alphabetic Filing, given before, and the sample question given below.

SAMPLE QUESTION

	Column I		Column II
w.	Doris Jenkin	A.	w, y, z, x
x.	Donald F. Jenkins	B.	y, w, z, x
y.	Donald Jenkin	C.	x, y, w, z
z.	D. Jenkins	D.	x, w, y, z

The correct way to enter these names is:

y. Donald Jenkin
w. Doris Jenkin
z. D. Jenkins
x. Donald F. Jenkins

The correct order is shown by the letters y, w, z, x, in that sequence. Since, in Column II, B appears in front of the letters y, w, z, x, in that sequence, B is the correct answer to the sample question.

Now answer the following questions using the same procedure.

		Column I		Column II	
1.	w.	Lawrence Robertson	A.	x, y, w, z	1.____
	x.	Jack L. Robinson	B.	w, z, x, y	
	y.	John Robinson	C.	z, w, x, y	
	z.	William B. Roberson	D.	z, w, y, x	
2.	w.	P. N. Figueredo	A.	y, x, z, w	2.____
	x.	M. Alice Figueroa	B.	x, z, w, y	
	y.	Jose Figueredo	C.	x, w, z, y	
	z.	M. Alicia Figueroa	D.	y, w, x, z	
3.	w.	George Steven Keats	A.	y, x, w, z	3.____
	x.	George S. Keats	B.	z, y, x, w	
	y.	G. Samuel Keats	C.	x, z, w, y	
	z.	Dr. Samuel Keats	D.	w, z, x, y	
4.	w.	V. Merchant	A.	w, x, y, z	4.____
	x.	Dr. William Mercher	B.	w, y, z, x	
	y.	Prof. Victor Merchant	C.	z, y, w, x	
	z.	Dr. Walter Merchan	D.	z, w, y, x	
5.	w.	Brian McCoy	A.	z, x, y, w	5.____
	x.	William Coyne	B.	y, w, z, x	
	y.	Mr. William MacCoyle	C.	x, z, y, w	
	z.	Dr. D. V. Coyne	D.	w, y, z, x	

6.
   w. Ms. M. Rosie Buchanan   A. z, y, x, w

   x. Rosalyn M. Buchanan   B. w, z, x, y

   y. Rosie Maria Buchanan   C. w, z, y, x

   z. Rosa Marie Buchanan   D. z, x, y, w

6.____

7.
   w. Prof. Jonathan Praga   A. w, z, y, x

   x. Dr. Joan Prager   B. w, x, z, y

   y. Alan VanPrague   C. x, w, z, y

   z. Alexander Prague   D. x, w, y, z

7.____

KEY (CORRECT ANSWERS)

1. C
2. D
3. A
4. D
5. A
6. B
7. B

TEST 3

DIRECTIONS: Questions 1 through 10 each show in Column I names written on four cards (lettered w, x, y, z) which have to be filed. You are to choose the option (lettered A, B, C, or D) in Column II which *BEST* represents the proper order of filing according to the rules and sample question given below. The cards are to be filed according to the Rules for Alphabetical Filing, given before, and the sample question given below.

SAMPLE QUESTION

	Column I		Column II
w.	Jane Earl	A.	w, y, z, x
x.	James A. Earle	B.	y, w, z, x
y.	James Earl	C.	x, y, w, z
z.	J. Earle	D.	x, w, y, z

The correct way to file the cards is:

y.	James Earl
w.	Jane Earl
z.	J. Earle
x.	James A. Earle

The correct filing order is shown by the letters y, w, z, x (in that order). Since, in Column II, B appears in front of the letters y, w, z, x (in that order), B is the correct answer to the sample question.

Now answer Questions 1 through 10 using the same procedure.

		Column I		Column II		
1.	w.	John Smith	A.	w, x, y, z	1.____
	x.	Joan Smythe	B.	y, z, x, w	
	y.	Gerald Schmidt	C.	y, z, w, x	
	z.	Gary Schmitt	D.	z, y, w, x	
2.	w.	A. Black	A.	w, x, y, z	2.____
	x.	Alan S. Black	B.	w, y, x, z	
	y.	Allan Black	C.	w, y, z, x	
	z.	Allen A. Black	D.	x, w, y, z	
3.	w.	Samuel Haynes	A.	w, x, y, z	3.____
	x.	Sam C. Haynes	B.	x, w, z, y	
	y.	David Haynes	C.	y, z, w, x	
	z.	Dave L. Haynes	D.	z, y, x, w	
4.	w.	Lisa B. McNeil	A.	x, y, w, z	4.____
	x.	Tom MacNeal	B.	x, z, y, w	
	y.	Lisa McNeil	C.	y, w, z, x	
	z.	Lorainne McNeal	D.	z, x, y, w	
5.	w.	Larry Richardson	A.	w, y, x, z	5.____
	x.	Leroy Richards	B.	y, x, z, w	
	y.	Larry S. Richards	C.	y, z, x, w	
	z.	Leroy C. Richards	D.	x, w, z, y	

6.	w.	Arlene Lane	A.	w, z, y, x
	x.	Arlene Cora Lane	B.	w, z, x, y
	y.	Arlene Clair Lane	C.	y, x, z, w
	z.	Arlene C. Lane	D.	z, y, w, x

6.___

7.	w.	Betty Fish	A.	w, x, z, y
	x.	Prof. Ann Fish	B.	x, w, y, z
	y.	Norma Fisch	C.	y, z, x, w
	z.	Dr. Richard Fisch	D.	z, y, w, x

7.___

8.	w.	Dr. Anthony David Lukak	A.	w, y, z, x
	x.	Mr. Steven Charles Lucas	B.	x, z, w, y
	y.	Mr. Anthony J. Lukak	C.	z, x, y, w
	z.	Prof. Steven C. Lucas	D.	z, x, w, y

8.___

9.	w.	Martha Y. Lind	A.	w, y, z, x
	x.	Mary Beth Linden	B.	w, y, x, z
	y.	Martha W. Lind	C.	y, w, z, x
	z.	Mary Bertha Linden	D.	y, w, x, z

9.___

10.	w.	Prof. Harry Michael MacPhelps	A.	w, z, x, y
	x.	Mr. Horace M. MacPherson	B.	w, y, z, x
	y.	Mr. Harold M. McPhelps	C.	z, x, w, y
	z.	Prof. Henry Martin MacPherson	D.	x, z, y, w

10.___

KEY (CORRECT ANSWERS)

1.	C	6.	A
2.	A	7.	C
3.	D	8.	D
4.	B	9.	C
5.	B	10.	A

TEST 4

DIRECTIONS: Answer Questions 1 through 5 on the basis of the following information:

A certain shop keeps an informational card file on all suppliers and merchandise. On each card is the supplier's name, the contract number for the merchandise he supplies, and a delivery date for the merchandise. In this filing system, the supplier's name is filed alphabetically, the contract number for the merchandise is filed numerically, and the delivery date is filed chronologically.

In Questions 1 through 5 there are five notations numbered 1 through 5 shown in Column I. Each notation is made up of a supplier's name, a contract number, and a date which is to be filed according to the following rules:

    First: File in alphabetical order;
    Second: When two or more notations have the same supplier, file according to the contract number in numerical order beginning with the lowest number;
    Third: When two or more notations have the same supplier and contract number, file according to the date beginning with the earliest date.

In Column II the numbers 1 through 5 are arranged in four ways to show four different orders in which the merchandise information might be filed. Pick the answer (A., B, C, or D) in Column II in which the notations are arranged according to the above filing rules.

SAMPLE QUESTION

Column I			Column II	
1.	Cluney	(4865) 6/17/02	A.	2, 3, 4, 1, 5
2.	Roster	(2466) 5/10/01	B.	2, 5, 1, 3, 4
3.	Altool	(7114) 10/15/02	C.	3, 2, 1, 4, 5
4.	Cluney	(5296) 12/18/01	D.	3, 5, 1, 4, 2
5.	Cluney	(4865) 4/8/02		

The correct way to file the cards is:
    3.   Altool (7114) 10/15/02
    5.   Cluney (4865) 4/8/02
    1.   Cluney (4865) 6/17/02
    4.   Cluney (5276) 12/18/01
    2.   Roster (2466) 5/10/01

Since the correct filing order is 3, 5, 1, 4, 2, the answer to the sample question is D. Now answer Questions 1 through 5.

		Column I				Column II	
1.	1.	warren	(96063)	3/30/03	A.	2, 4, 3, 5, 1	1.____
	2.	moore	(21237)	9/4/04	B.	2, 3, 5, 4, 1	
	3.	newman	(10050)	12/12/03	C.	4, 5, 2, 3, 1	
	4.	downs	(81251)	1/2/03	D.	4, 2, 3, 5, 1	
	5.	oliver	(60145)	6/30/04			

2.
1.	Henry	(40552)	7/6/04		A.	5, 4, 3, 1, 2
2.	Boyd	(91251)	9/1/03		B.	2, 3, 4, 1, 5
3.	George	(8196)	12/12/03		C.	2, 4, 3, 1, 5
4.	George	(31096)	1/12/04		D.	5, 2, 3, 1, 4
5.	West	(6109)	8/9/03			

2.___

3.
1.	Salba	(4670)	9/7/03		A.	5, 3, 1, 2, 4
2.	Salba	(51219)	3/1/03		B.	3, 1, 2, 4, 5
3.	Crete	(81562)	7/1/04		C.	3, 5, 4, 2, 1
4.	Salba	(51219)	1/11/04		D.	5, 3, 4, 2, 1
5.	Texi	(31549)	1/25/03			

3.___

4.
1.	Crayone	(87105)	6/10/04		A.	1, 2, 5, 3, 4
2.	Shamba	(49210)	1/5/03		B.	1, 5, 2, 3, 4
3.	Valiant	(3152)	5/1/04		C.	1, 5, 3, 4, 2
4.	Valiant	(3152)	1/9/04		D.	1, 5, 2, 4, 3
5.	Poro	(59613)	7/1/03			

4.___

5.
1.	Mackie	(42169)	12/20/03		A.	3, 2, 1, 5, 4
2.	Lebo	(5198)	9/12/02		B.	3, 2, 4, 5, 1
3.	Drummon	(99631)	9/9/04		C.	3, 5, 2, 4, 1
4.	Lebo	(15311)	1/25/02		D.	3, 5, 4, 2, 1
5.	Harvin	(81765)	6/2/03			

5.___

KEY (CORRECT ANSWERS)

1.	D
2.	B
3.	B
4.	D
5.	C

TEST 5

DIRECTIONS: Each of Questions 1 through 8 represents five cards to be filed, numbered 1 through 5 in Column I. Each card is made up of the employee's name, the date of a work assignment, and the work assignment code number shown in parentheses. The cards are to be filed according to the following rules:

First: File in alphabetical order;
Second: When two or more cards have the same employee's name, file according to the assignment date beginning with the earliest date;
Third: When two or more cards have the same employee's name and the same date, file according to the work assignment number beginning with the lowest number.

Column II shows the cards arranged in four different orders. Pick the answer (A, B, C, or D) in Column II which shows the cards arranged correctly according to the above filing rules.

SAMPLE QUESTION

	Column I				Column II
1.	Cluney	4/8/02	(486503)	A.	2, 3, 4, 1, 5
2.	Roster	5/10/01	(246611)	B.	2, 5, 1, 3, 4
3.	Altool	10/15/02	(711433)	C.	3, 2, 1, 4, 5
4.	Cluney	12/18/02	(527610)	D.	3, 5, 1, 4, 2
5.	Cluney	4/8/02	(486500)		

The correct way to file the cards is:
    3.   Altool 10/15/02 (711433)
    5.   Cluney 4/8/02 (486500)
    1.   Cluney 4/8/02 (486503)
    4.   Cluney 12/18/02 (527610)
    2.   Roster 5/10/01 (246611)

The correct filing order is shown by the numbers in front of each name (3, 5, 1, 4, 2). The answer to the sample question is the letter in Column II in front of the numbers 3, 5, 1, 4, 2. This answer is D.

Now answer Questions 1 through 8 according to these rules.

1.								
	1.	Kohls	4/2/02	(125677)	A.	1, 2, 3, 4, 5		1._____
	2.	Keller	3/21/02	(129698)	B.	3, 2, 1, 4, 5		
	3.	Jackson	4/10/02	(213541)	C.	3, 1, 2, 4, 5		
	4.	Richards	1/9/03	(347236)	D.	5, 2, 1, 3, 4		
	5.	Richmond	12/11/01	(379321)				

2.								
	1.	Burroughs	5/27/02	(237896)	A.	1, 4, 3, 2, 5		2._____
	2.	Charlson	1/16/02	(114537)	B.	4, 1, 5, 3, 2		
	3.	Carlsen	12/2/02	(114377)	C.	1, 4, 3, 5, 2		
	4.	Burton	5/1/02	(227096)	D.	4, 1, 3, 5, 2		
	5.	Charlson	12/2/02	(114357)				

3.	A.	Ungerer	11/11/02	(537924)		A.	1, 5, 3, 2, 4		3._
	B.	Winters	1/10/02	(657834)		B.	5, 1, 3, 4, 2		
	C.	Ventura	12/1/02	(698694)		C.	3, 5, 1, 2, 4		
	D.	Winters	10/11/02	(675654)		D.	1, 5, 3, 4, 2		
	E.	Ungaro	1/10/02	(684325)					

4.	1.	Norton	3/12/03	(071605)		A.	1, 4, 2, 3, 5		4._
	2.	Morris	2/26/03	(068931)		B.	3, 5, 2, 4, 1		
	3.	Morse	5/12/03	(142358)		C.	2, 4, 3, 5, 1		
	4.	Morris	2/26/03	(068391)		D.	4, 2, 5, 3, 1		
	5.	Morse	2/26/03	(068391)					

5.	1.	Eger	4/19/02	(874129)		A.	3, 4, 1, 2, 5		5._
	2.	Eihler	5/19/03	(875329)		B.	1, 4, 5, 2, 3		
	3.	Ehrlich	11/19/02	(874839)		C.	4, 1, 3, 2, 5		
	4.	Eger	4/19/02	(876129)		D.	1, 4, 3, 5, 2		
	5.	Eihler	5/19/02	(874239)					

6.	1.	Johnson	12/21/02	(786814)		A.	2, 4, 3, 5, 1		6._
	2.	Johns	12/21/03	(801024)		B.	4, 2, 5, 3, 1		
	3.	Johnson	12/12/03	(762814)		C.	4, 5, 3, 1, 2		
	4.	Jackson	12/12/03	(862934)		D.	5, 3, 1, 2, 4		
	5.	Johnson	12/12/03	(762184)					

7.	1.	Fuller	7/12/02	(598310)		A.	2, 1, 5, 4, 3		7._
	2.	Fuller	7/2/02	(598301)		B.	1, 2, 4, 5, 3		
	3.	Fuller	7/22/02	(598410)		C.	1, 4, 5, 2, 3		
	4.	Fuller	7/17/03	(598710)		D.	2, 1, 3, 5, 4		
	5.	Fuller	7/17/03	(598701)					

8.	1.	Perrine	10/27/99	(637096)		A.	3, 4, 5, 1, 2		8._
	2.	Perrone	11/14/02	(767609)		B.	3, 2, 5, 4, 1		
	3.	Perrault	10/15/98	(629706)		C.	5, 3, 4, 1, 2		
	4.	Perrine	10/17/02	(373656)		D.	4, 5, 1, 2, 3		
	5.	Perine	10/17/01	(376356)					

KEY (CORRECT ANSWERS)

1. B
2. A
3. B
4. D
5. D
6. B
7. D
8. C

TEST 6

DIRECTIONS: Each question or incomplete statement is followed by several suggested answers or completions. Select the one that *BEST* answers the question or completes the statement. *PRINT THE LETTER OF THE CORRECT ANSWER IN THE SPACE AT THE RIGHT.*

1. Which one of the following *BEST* describes the usual arrangement of a tickler file?   1.____

    A. Alphabetical   B. Chronological
    C. Numerical   D. Geographical

2. Which one of the following is the *LEAST* desirable filing practice?   2.____

    A. Using staples to keep papers together
    B. Filing all material without regard to date
    C. Keeping a record of all materials removed from the files
    D. Writing filing instructions on each paper prior to filing

3. The one of the following records which it would be *MOST* advisable to keep in alphabetical order is a   3.____

    A. continuous listing of phone messages, including time and caller, for your supervisor
    B. listing of individuals currently employed by your agency in a particular title
    C. record of purchases paid for by the petty cash fund
    D. dated record of employees who have borrowed material from the files in your office

4. Tickler systems are used in many legal offices for scheduling and calendar control. Of the following, the *LEAST* common use of a tickler system is to   4.____

    A. keep papers filed in such a way that they may easily be retrieved
    B. arrange for the appearance of witnesses when they will be needed
    C. remind lawyers when certain papers are due
    D. arrange for the gathering of certain types of evidence

5. A type of file which permits the operator to remain seated while the file can be moved backward and forward as required is *BEST* termed a   5.____

    A. lateral file   B. movable file
    C. reciprocating file   D. rotary file

6. In which of the following cases would it be *MOST* desirable to have two cards for one individual in a single alphabetic file? The individual has   6.____

    A. a hyphenated surname
    B. two middle names
    C. a first name with an unusual spelling
    D. a compound first name

KEY (CORRECT ANSWERS)

1. B
2. B
3. B
4. A
5. C
6. A

———

CLERICAL ABILITIES TEST

Clerical aptitude involves the ability to perceive pertinent detail in verbal or tabular material, to observe differences in copy, to proofread words and numbers, and to avoid perceptual errors in arithmetic computation.

NATURE OF THE TEST

Four types of clerical aptitude questions are presented in the Clerical Abilities Test. There are 120 questions with a short time limit. The test contains 30 questions on name and number checking, 30 on the arrangement of names in correct alphabetical order, 30 on simple arithmetic, and 30 on inspecting groups of letters and numbers. The questions have been arranged in groups or cycles of five questions of each type. The Clerical Abilities Test is primarily a test of speed in carrying out relatively simple clerical tasks. While accuracy on these tasks is important and will be taken into account in the scoring, experience has shown that many persons are so concerned about accuracy that they do the test more slowly than they should. Competitors should be cautioned that speed as well as accuracy is important to achieve a good score.

HOW THE TEST IS ADMINISTERED

Each competitor should be given a copy of the test booklet with sample questions on the cover page, an answer sheet, and a medium No. 2 pencil. Ten minutes are allowed to study the directions and sample questions and to answer the questions in the proper boxes on the two pages.

The separate answer sheet should be used for the test proper. Fifteen minutes are allowed for the test.

HOW THE TEST IS SCORED

The correct answers should be counted and recorded. The number of incorrect answers must also be counted because one-fourth of the number of incorrect answers is subtracted from the number of right answers. An omission is considered as neither a right nor a wrong answer. The score on this test is the number of right answers minus one-fourth of the number of wrong answers (fractions of one-half or less are dropped). For example, if an applicant had answered 89 questions correctly and 10 questions incorrectly, and had omitted 1 question, his score would be 87.

EXAMINATION SECTION

DIRECTIONS: This test contains four kinds of questions. There are some of each kind on each page in the booklet. The time limit for the test will be announced by the examiner.

Use the special pencil furnished by the examiner in marking your answers on the separate answer sheet. For each question, there are five suggested answers. Decide which answer is correct, find the number of the question on the answer sheet, and make a *solid black mark* between the dotted lines just below the letter of your answer. If you wish to change your answer, erase the first mark completely—do not merely cross it out.

SAMPLE QUESTIONS

In each line across the page there are three names or numbers that are much alike. Compare the three names or numbers and decide which ones are exactly alike. On the Sample Answer Sheet at the right, mark the answer-

A   if ALL THREE names or numbers are exactly ALIKE
B   if only the FIRST and SECOND names or numbers are exactly ALIKE
C   if only the FIRST and THIRD names or numbers are exactly ALIKE
D   if only the SECOND and THIRD names or numbers are exactly ALIKE
E   if ALL THREE names or numbers are DIFFERENT

I.	Davis Hazen	David Hozen	David Hazen
II.	Lois Appel	Lois Appel	Lois Apfel
III.	June Allan	Jane Allan	Jane Allan
IV.	10235	10235	10235
V.	32614	32164	32614

SAMPLE ANSWER SHEET				
	A	B	C	D	E

	A	B	C	D	E
I	∷	∷	∷	∷	∷
II	∷	∷	∷	∷	∷
III	∷	∷	∷	∷	∷
IV	∷	∷	∷	∷	∷
V	∷	∷	∷	∷	∷
VI	∷	∷	∷	∷	∷
VII	∷	∷	∷	∷	∷

It will be to your advantage to learn what A, B, C, D, and E stand for. If you finish the sample questions before you are told to turn to the test, study them.

In the next group of sample questions, there is a name in a box at the left, and four other names in alphabetical order at the right. Find the correct space for the boxed name so that it will be in alphabetical order with the others, and mark the letter of that space as your answer.

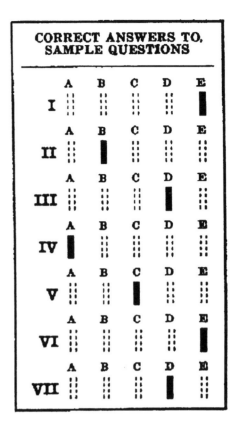

CORRECT ANSWERS TO.
SAMPLE QUESTIONS

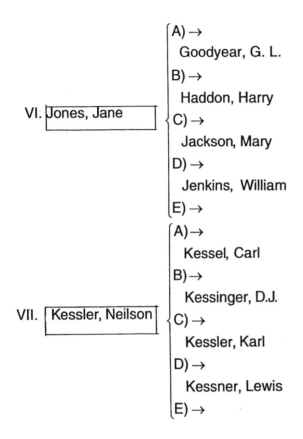

VI. Jones, Jane

A) →
  Goodyear, G. L.
B) →
  Haddon, Harry
C) →
  Jackson, Mary
D) →
  Jenkins, William
E) →

VII. Kessler, Neilson

A) →
  Kessel, Carl
B) →
  Kessinger, D.J.
C) →
  Kessler, Karl
D) →
  Kessner, Lewis
E) →

DIRECTIONS: In the following questions, complete the equation and find your answer among the list of suggested answers. Mark the Sample Answer Sheet A, B, C or D for the answer you obtained; or if your answer is not among these, mark E for that question.

VIII. Add:

   22   A) 44 B) 45
+ 33   C) 54 D) 55
         E) none of these

X. Multiply:

   25   A) 100 B) 115
x 5   C) 125 D) 135
        E) none of these

IX. Subtract:

   24   A) 20 B) 21
− 3   C) 27 D) 29
        E) none of these

XI. Divide:

           A) 20 B) 22
6 / 126 C) 24 D) 26
        E) none of these

4

Directions: There is one set of suggested answers for the next group of sample questions. Do not try to memorize these answers, because there will be a different set on each page in the test.

To find the answer to a question, find which suggested answer contains numbers and letters all of which appear in the question. If no suggested answer fits, mark E for that question.

XII. 8NK9GT46
XIII. T97Z6L3K
XIV. Z7GK398N
XV. 3K946GZL
XVI. ZN738KT9

Suggested Answers
A = 7,9,G,K
B = 8,9,T,Z
C = 6,7,K,Z
D = 6,8,G,T
E = none of these

	SAMPLE ANSWER SHEET						CORRECT ANSWERS TO SAMPLE QUESTIONS				
	A	B	C	D	E		A	B	C	D	E
VIII						VIII				■	
IX						IX		■			
X						X			■		
XI						XI					■
XII						XII				■	
XIII						XIII		■			
XIV						XIV	■				
XV						XV					■
XVI						XVI	■				

After you have marked your answers to all the questions on the Sample Answer Sheets on this page and on the front page of the booklet, check them with the answers in the boxes marked Correct Answers to Sample Questions.

In questions 1 through 5, compare the three names or numbers, and mark

A if ALL THREE names or numbers are exactly ALIKE
B if only the FIRST and SECOND names or numbers are exactly ALIKE
C if only the FIRST and THIRD names or numbers are exactly ALIKE
D if only the SECOND and THIRD names or numbers are exactly ALIKE
E if ALL THREE names or numbers are DIFFERENT

1. 5261383   5261383   5261338
2. 8125690   8126690   8125609
3. W. E. Johnston   W. E. Johnson   W. E. Johnson
4. Vergil L. Muller   Vergil L. Muller   Vergil L. Muller
5. Atherton R. Warde   Asheton R. Warde   Atherton P. Warde

138

In questions 6 through 10, find the correct place for the name in the box.

6. Hackett, Gerald

A) →
Habert, James
B) →
Hachett, J. J.
C) →
Hachetts, K, Larson
D) →
Hachettson, Leroy
E) →

7. Margenroth, Alvin

A) →
Margeroth, Albert
B) →
Margestein, Dan
C) →
Margestein, David
D) →
Margue, Edgar
E) →

8. Bobbitt, Olivier E.

A) →
Bobbitt, D. Olivier
B) →
Bobbitt, Olive B.
C) →
Bobbitt, Olivia H.
D) →
Bobbitt, R. Olivia
E) →

9. Mosely, Werner

A) →
Mosely, Albert J.
B) →
Mosley, Alvin
C) →
Mosley, S. M.
D) →
Mozley, Vinson N.
E) →

10. Youmuns, Frank L.

A) →
Youmons, Frank G.
B) →
Youmons, Frank H.
C) →
Youmons, Frank K.
D) →
Youmons, Frank M.
E) →

GO ON TO THE NEXT COLUMN.

Answers

11. Add:

4 3
+ 3 2
——

A) 55 B) 65
C) 66 D) 75
E) none of these

12. Subtract:

8 3
−   4
——

A) 73 B) 79
C) 80 D) 89
E) none of these

13. Multiply:

4 1
×   7
——

A) 281 B) 287
C) 291 D) 297
E) none of these

14. Divide:

6 / 3 0 6

A) 44 B) 51
C) 52 D) 60
E) none of these

15. Add:

3 7
+ 1 5
——

A) 42 B) 52
C) 53 D) 62
E) none of these

For each question below, find which one of the suggested answers appears in that question.

16. 6 2 5 K 4 P T G

17. L 4 7 2 T 6 V K

18. 3 5 4 L 9 V T G

19. G 4 K 7 L 3 5 Z

20. 4 K 2 9 N 5 T G

Suggested Answers

A = 4, 5, K, T
B = 4, 7, G, K
C = 2, 5, G, L
D = 2, 7, L, T
E = none of these

GO ON TO THE NEXT PAGE.

In questions 21 through 25, compare the three names or numbers, and mark the answer

A   if ALL THREE names or numbers are exactly ALIKE
B   if only the FIRST and SECOND names or numbers are exactly ALIKE
C   if only the FIRST and THIRD names or numbers are exactly ALIKE
D   if only the SECOND and THIRD names or numbers are exactly ALIKE
E   if ALL THREE names or numbers are DIFFERENT

21. 2395890	2395890	2395890
22. 1926341	1926347	1926314
23. E. Owens McVey	E. Owen McVey	E. Owen McVay
24. Emily Neal Rouse	Emily Neal Rowse	Emily Neal Rowse
25. H. Merritt Audubon	H. Merriott Audubon	H. Merritt Audubon

In questions 26 through 30, find the correct place for the name in the box.

26. | Watters, N. O. |
A) →
Waters, Charles L.
B) →
Waterson, Nina P.
C) →
Watson, Nora J.
D) →
Wattwood, Paul A.
E) →

27. | Johnston, Edward |
A) →
Johnston, Edgar R.
B) →
Johnston, Edmond
C) →
Johnston, Edmund
D) →
Johnstone, Edmund A.
E) →

28. | Rensch, Adeline |
A) →
Ramsay, Amos
B) →
Remschel, Augusta
C) →
Renshaw, Austin
D) →
Rentzel, Becky
E) →

29. | Schnyder, Maurice |
A) →
Schneider, Martin
B) →
Schneider, Mertens
C) →
Schnyder, Newman
D) →
Schreibner, Norman
E) →

30. | Freedenburg, C. Erma |
A) →
Freedenberg, Emerson
B) →
Freedenberg, Erma
C) →
Freedenberg, Erma E.
D) →
Freedinberg, Erma F.
E) →

GO ON TO THE NEXT COLUMN.

Answers

→ 31. Subtract:
$$\begin{array}{r} 6\ 8 \\ -\ 4\ 7 \\ \hline \end{array}$$
A) 10   B) 11
C) 20   D) 22
E) none of these

32. Multiply:
$$\begin{array}{r} 5\ 0 \\ \times\quad 8 \\ \hline \end{array}$$
A) 400   B) 408
C) 450   D) 458
E) none of these

33. Divide:
$$9\,\overline{)\,1\ 8\ 0}$$
A) 20   B) 29
C) 30   D) 39
E) none of these

34. Add:
$$\begin{array}{r} 7\ 8 \\ +\ 6\ 3 \\ \hline \end{array}$$
A) 131   B) 140
C) 141   D) 151
E) none of these

35. Subtract:
$$\begin{array}{r} 8\ 9 \\ -\ 7\ 0 \\ \hline \end{array}$$
A) 9   B) 18
C) 19   D) 29
E) none of these

For each question below, find which one of the suggested answers appears in that question.

36. 9 G Z 3 L 4 6 N

37. L 5 N K 4 3 9 V

38. 8 2 V P 9 L Z 5

39. V P 9 Z 5 L 8 7

40. 5 T 8 N 2 9 V L

Suggested Answers
A = 4, 9, L, V
B = 4, 5, N, Z
C = 5, 8, L, Z
D = 8, 9, N, V
E = none of these

GO ON TO THE NEXT PAGE.

In questions 41 through 45, compare the three names or numbers, and mark the answer

A   if ALL THREE names or numbers are exactly ALIKE
B   if only the FIRST and SECOND names or numbers are exactly ALIKE
C   if only the FIRST and THIRD names or numbers are exactly ALIKE
D   if only the SECOND and THIRD names or numbers are exactly ALIKE
E   if ALL THREE names or numbers are DIFFERENT

41. 6219354	6219354	6219354
42. 2312793	2312793	2312793
43. 1065407	1065407	1065047
44. Francis Ransdell	Frances Ramsdell	Francis Ramsdell
45. Cornelius Detwiler	Cornelius Detwiler	Cornelius Detwiler

In questions 46 through 50, find the correct place for the name in the box.

46. **DeMattia, Jessica**

A) →
DeLong, Jesse
B) →
DeMatteo, Jessie
C) →
Derby, Jessie S.
D) →
DeShazo, L. M.
E) →

47. **Theriault, Louis**

A) →
Therien, Annette
B) →
Therien, Elaine
C) →
Thibeault, Gerald
D) →
Thiebeault, Pierre
E) →

48. **Gaston, M. Hubert**

A) →
Gaston, Dorothy M.
B) →
Gaston, Henry N.
C) →
Gaston, Isabel
D) →
Gaston, M. Melvin
E) →

49. **SanMiguel, Carlos**

A) →
SanLuis, Juana
B) →
Santilli, Laura
C) →
Stinnett, Nellie
D) →
Stoddard, Victor
E) →

50. **DeLaTour, Hall F.**

A) →
Delargy, Harold
B) →
DeLathouder, Hilda
C) →
Lathrop, Hillary
D) →
LaTour, Hulbert E.
E) →

GO ON TO THE NEXT COLUMN.

Answers

→ 51. Multiply:
6 2
× 5
——

A) 300   B) 310
C) 315   D) 360
E) none of these

52. Divide:

3 / 1 5 3

A) 41   B) 43
C) 51   D) 53
E) none of these

53. Add:
4 7
+ 2 1
——

A) 58   B) 59
C) 67   D) 68
E) none of these

54. Subtract:
8 7
− 4 2
——

A) 34   B) 35
C) 44   D) 45
E) none of these

55. Multiply:
3 7
× 3
——

A) 91   B) 101
C) 104   D) 114
E) none of these

For each question below, find which one of the suggested answers appears in that question.

56. N 5 4 7 T K 3 Z

57. 8 5 3 V L 2 Z N

58. 7 2 5 N 9 K L V

59. 9 8 L 2 5 Z K V

60. Z 6 5 V 9 3 P N

Suggested Answers
A = 3, 8, K, N
B = 5, 8, N, V
C = 3, 9, V, Z
D = 5, 9, K, Z
E = none of these

GO ON TO THE NEXT PAGE.

In questions 61 through 65, compare the three names or numbers, and mark the answer

A   if ALL THREE names or numbers are exactly ALIKE
B   if only the FIRST and SECOND names or numbers are exactly ALIKE
C   if only the FIRST and THIRD names or numbers are exactly ALIKE
D   if only the SECOND and THIRD names or numbers are exactly ALIKE
E   if ALL THREE names or numbers are DIFFERENT

61.	6452054	6452654	6452054
62.	8501268	8501268	8501286
63.	Ella Burk Newham	Ella Burk Newnham	Elena Burk Newnham
64.	Jno. K. Ravencroft	Jno. H. Ravencroft	Jno. H. Ravencoft
65.	Martin Wills Pullen	Martin Wills Pulen	Martin Wills Pullen

In questions 66 through 70, find the correct place for the name in the box.

66. | O'Bannon, M. J. |
A) →
  O'Beirne, B. B.
B) →
  Oberlin, E. L.
C) →
  Oberneir, L. P.
D) →
  O'Brian, S. F.
E) →

67. | Entsminger, Jacob |
A) →
  Ensminger, J.
B) →
  Entsminger, J. A.
C) →
  Entsminger, Jack
D) →
  Entsminger, James
E) →

68. | Iacone, Pete R. |
A) →
  Iacone, Pedro
B) →
  Iacone, Pedro M.
C) →
  Iacone, Peter F.
D) →
  Iascone, Peter W.
E) →

69. | Sheppard, Gladys |
A) →
  Shepard, Dwight
B) →
  Shepard, F. H.
C) →
  Shephard, Louise
D) →
  Shepperd, Stella
E) →

70. | Thackton, Melvin T. |
A) →
  Thackston, Milton G.
B) →
  Thackston, Milton W.
C) →
  Thackston, Theodore
D) →
  Thackston, Thomas G.
E) →

GO ON TO THE NEXT COLUMN.

Answers

71. Divide:

$7 \overline{\smash{)}357}$

A) 51   B) 52
C) 53   D) 54
E) none of these

72. Add:

  5 8
+ 2 7

A) 75   B) 84
C) 85   D) 95
E) none of these

73. Subtract:

  8 6
− 5 7

A) 18   B) 29
C) 38   D) 39
E) none of these

74. Multiply:

  6 8
×   4

A) 242   B) 264
C) 272   D) 274
E) none of these

75. Divide:

$9 \overline{\smash{)}639}$

A) 71   B) 73
C) 81   D) 83
E) none of these

For each question below, find which one of the suggested answers appears in that question.

76.   6 Z T N 8 7 4 V

77.   V 7 8 6 N 5 P L

78.   N 7 P V 8 4 2 L

79.   7 8 G 4 3 V L T

80.   4 8 G 2 T N 6 L

Suggested Answers
A = 2, 7, L, N
B = 2, 8, T, V
C = 6, 8, L, T
D = 6, 7, N, V
E = none of these

GO ON TO THE NEXT PAGE.

In questions 81 through 85, compare the three names or numbers, and mark the answer

A   if ALL THREE names or numbers are exactly ALIKE
B   if only the FIRST and SECOND names or numbers are exactly ALIKE
C   if only the FIRST and THIRD names or numbers are exactly ALIKE
D   if only the SECOND and THIRD names or numbers are exactly ALIKE
E   if ALL THREE names or numbers are DIFFERENT

81. 3457988   3457986   3457986
82. 4695682   4695862   4695682
83. Stricklund Kanedy   Stricklund Kanedy   Stricklund Kanedy
84. Joy Harlor Witner   Joy Harloe Witner   Joy Harloe Witner
85. R. M. O. Uberroth   R. M. O. Uberroth   R. N. O. Uberroth

In questions 86 through 90, find the correct place for the name in the box.

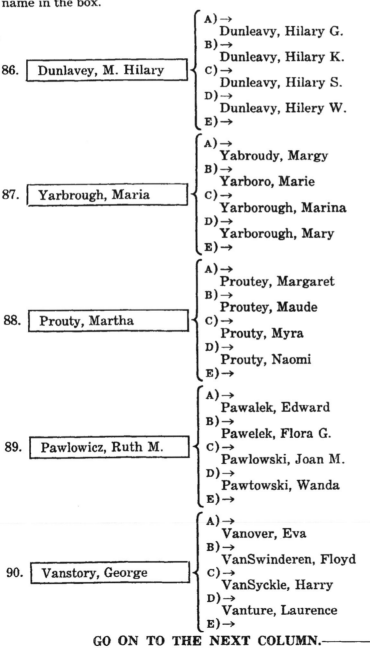

86. │ Dunlavey, M. Hilary │
A)→
   Dunleavy, Hilary G.
B)→
   Dunleavy, Hilary K.
C)→
   Dunleavy, Hilary S.
D)→
   Dunleavy, Hilery W.
E)→

87. │ Yarbrough, Maria │
A)→
   Yabroudy, Margy
B)→
   Yarboro, Marie
C)→
   Yarborough, Marina
D)→
   Yarborough, Mary
E)→

88. │ Prouty, Martha │
A)→
   Proutey, Margaret
B)→
   Proutey, Maude
C)→
   Prouty, Myra
D)→
   Prouty, Naomi
E)→

89. │ Pawlowicz, Ruth M. │
A)→
   Pawalek, Edward
B)→
   Pawelek, Flora G.
C)→
   Pawlowski, Joan M.
D)→
   Pawtowski, Wanda
E)→

90. │ Vanstory, George │
A)→
   Vanover, Eva
B)→
   VanSwinderen, Floyd
C)→
   VanSyckle, Harry
D)→
   Vanture, Laurence
E)→

Answers

→ 91. Add:
       2 8
     + 3 5
     ——

A) 53   B) 62
C) 64   D) 73
E) none of these

92. Subtract:
       7 8
     − 6 9
     ——

A) 7   B) 8
C) 18   D) 19
E) none of these

93. Multiply:
       8 6
     ×   6
     ——

A) 492 B) 506
C) 516 D) 526
E) none of these

94. Divide:

     8 / 6 4 8

A) 71   B) 76
C) 81   D) 89
E) none of these

95. Add:
       9 7
     + 3 4
     ——

A) 131 B) 132
C) 140 D) 141
E) none of these

For each question below, find which one of the suggested answers appears in that question.

96. V 5 7 Z N 9 4 T

97. 4 6 P T 2 N K 9

98. 6 4 N 2 P 8 Z K

99. 7 P 5 2 4 N K T

100. K T 8 5 4 N 2 P

Suggested Answers
A=2, 5, N, Z
B=4, 5, N, P
C=2, 9, P, T
D=4, 9, T, Z
E=none of these

GO ON TO THE NEXT COLUMN.————

GO ON TO THE NEXT PAGE.

In questions 101 through 105, compare the three names or numbers, and mark the answer

A   if ALL THREE names or numbers are exactly ALIKE
B   if only the FIRST and SECOND names or numbers are exactly ALIKE
C   if only the FIRST and THIRD names or numbers are exactly ALIKE
D   if only the SECOND and THIRD names or numbers are exactly ALIKE
E   if ALL THREE names or numbers are DIFFERENT

101.	1592514	1592574	1592574
102.	2010202	2010202	2010220
103.	6177396	6177936	6177396
104.	Drusilla S. Ridgeley	Drusilla S. Ridgeley	Drusilla S. Ridgeley
105.	Andrei I. Toumantzev	Andrei I. Tourmantzev	Andrei I. Toumantzov

In questions 106 through 110, find the correct place for the name in the box.

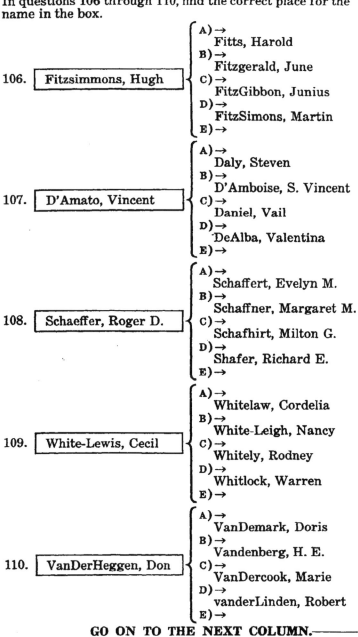

106. Fitzsimmons, Hugh
A)→ Fitts, Harold
B)→ Fitzgerald, June
C)→ FitzGibbon, Junius
D)→ FitzSimons, Martin
E)→

107. D'Amato, Vincent
A)→ Daly, Steven
B)→ D'Amboise, S. Vincent
C)→ Daniel, Vail
D)→ DeAlba, Valentina
E)→

108. Schaeffer, Roger D.
A)→ Schaffert, Evelyn M.
B)→ Schaffner, Margaret M.
C)→ Schafhirt, Milton G.
D)→ Shafer, Richard E.
E)→

109. White-Lewis, Cecil
A)→ Whitelaw, Cordelia
B)→ White-Leigh, Nancy
C)→ Whitely, Rodney
D)→ Whitlock, Warren
E)→

110. VanDerHeggen, Don
A)→ VanDemark, Doris
B)→ Vandenberg, H. E.
C)→ VanDercook, Marie
D)→ vanderLinden, Robert
E)→

GO ON TO THE NEXT COLUMN.

Answers

111. Add:
7 5
+ 4 9
A) 124 B) 125 C) 134 D) 225 E) none of these

112. Subtract:
6 9
− 4 5
A) 14 B) 23 C) 24 D) 26 E) none of these

113. Multiply:
3 6
× 8
A) 246 B) 262 C) 288 D) 368 E) none of these

114. Divide:
8 / 3 2 8
A) 31 B) 41 C) 42 D) 48 E) none of these

115. Multiply:
5 8
× 9
A) 472 B) 513 C) 521 D) 522 E) none of these

For each question below, find which one of the suggested answers appears in that question.

116. Z 3 N P G 5 4 2

117. 6 N 2 8 G 4 P T

118. 6 N 4 T V G 8 2

119. T 3 P 4 N 8 G 2

120. 6 7 K G N 2 L 5

Suggested Answers
A=2, 3, G, N
B=2, 6, N, T
C=3, 4, G, K
D=4, 6, K, T
E=none of these

KEY (CORRECT ANSWERS)

1. B	21. A	41. A	61. C	81. D	101. D
2. E	22. E	42. A	62. B	82. C	102. B
3. D	23. E	43. B	63. E	83. A	103. C
4. A	24. D	44. E	64. E	84. D	104. A
5. E	25. C	45. A	65. C	85. B	105. E
6. E	26. D	46. C	66. A	86. A	106. D
7. A	27. D	47. A	67. D	87. E	107. B
8. D	28. C	48. D	68. C	88. C	108. A
9. B	29. C	49. B	69. D	89. C	109. C
10. E	30. D	50. C	70. E	90. B	110. D
11. D	31. E	51. B	71. A	91. E	111. A
12. B	32. A	52. C	72. C	92. E	112. C
13. B	33. A	53. D	73. B	93. C	113. C
14. B	34. C	54. D	74. C	94. C	114. B
15. B	35. C	55. E	75. A	95. A	115. D
16. A	36. E	56. E	76. D	96. D	116. A
17. D	37. A	57. B	77. D	97. C	117. B
18. E	38. C	58. E	78. A	98. E	118. B
19. B	39. C	59. D	79. E	99. B	119. A
20. A	40. D	60. C	80. C	100. B	120. E

CLERICAL ABILITIES

EXAMINATION SECTION
TEST 1

DIRECTIONS: Each question or incomplete statement is followed by several suggested answers or completions. Select the one that BEST answers the question or completes the statement. *PRINT THE LETTER OF THE CORRECT ANSWER IN THE SPACE AT THE RIGHT.*

Questions 1-4.

DIRECTIONS: Questions 1 through 4 are to be answered on the basis of the information given below.

The most commonly used filing system and the one that is easiest to learn is alphabetical filing. This involves putting records in an A to Z order, according to the letters of the alphabet. The name of a person is filed by using the following order: first, the surname or last name; second, the first name; third, the middle name or middle initial. For example, *Henry C. Young* is filed under *Y* and thereafter under *Young, Henry C.* The name of a company is filed in the same way. For example, *Long Cabinet Co.* is filed under *L,* while *John T. Long Cabinet Co.* is filed under *L* and thereafter under *Long., John T. Cabinet Co.*

1. The one of the following which lists the names of persons in the CORRECT alphabetical order is:

    A. Mary Carrie, Helen Carrol, James Carson, John Carter
    B. James Carson, Mary Carrie, John Carter, Helen Carrol
    C. Helen Carrol, James Carson, John Carter, Mary Carrie
    D. John Carter, Helen Carrol, Mary Carrie, James Carson

1.____

2. The one of the following which lists the names of persons in the CORRECT alphabetical order is:

    A. Jones, John C.; Jones, John A.; Jones, John P.; Jones, John K.
    B. Jones, John P.; Jones, John K.; Jones, John C.; Jones, John A.
    C. Jones, John A.; Jones, John C.; Jones, John K.; Jones, John P.
    D. Jones, John K.; Jones, John C.; Jones, John A.; Jones, John P.

2.____

3. The one of the following which lists the names of the companies in the CORRECT alphabetical order is:

    A. Blane Co., Blake Co., Block Co., Blear Co.
    B. Blake Co., Blane Co., Blear Co., Block Co.
    C. Block Co., Blear Co., Blane Co., Blake Co.
    D. Blear Co., Blake Co., Blane Co., Block Co.

3.____

4. You are to return to the file an index card on *Barry C. Wayne Materials and Supplies Co.* Of the following, the CORRECT alphabetical group that you should return the index card to is

    A. A to G   B. H to M   C. N to S   D. T to Z

4.____

Questions 5-10.

DIRECTIONS: In each of Questions 5 through 10, the names of four people are given. For each question, choose as your answer the one of the four names given which should be filed FIRST according to the usual system of alphabetical filing of names, as described in the following paragraph.

In filing names, you must start with the last name. Names are filed in order of the first letter of the last name, then the second letter, etc. Therefore, BAILY would be filed before BROWN, which would be filed before COLT. A name with fewer letters of the same type comes first; i.e., Smith before Smithe. If the last names are the same, the names are filed alphabetically by the first name. If the first name is an initial, a name with an initial would come before a first name that starts with the same letter as the initial. Therefore, I. BROWN would come before IRA BROWN. Finally, if both last name and first name are the same, the name would be filed alphabetically by the middle name, once again an initial coming before a middle name which starts with the same letter as the initial. If there is no middle name at all, the name would come before those with middle initials or names.

Sample Question: A. Lester Daniels
　　　　　　　　　　 B. William Dancer
　　　　　　　　　　 C. Nathan Danzig
　　　　　　　　　　 D. Dan Lester

The last names beginning with D are filed before the last name beginning with L. Since DANIELS, DANCER, and DANZIG all begin with the same three letters, you must look at the fourth letter of the last name to determine which name should be filed first. C comes before I or Z in the alphabet, so DANCER is filed before DANIELS or DANZIG. Therefore, the answer to the above sample question is B.

5.　　A. Scott Biala　　　　　　　　　　　　　　　　　　　　　　　　　　　5._____
　　　 B. Mary Byala
　　　 C. Martin Baylor
　　　 D. Francis Bauer

6.　　A. Howard J. Black　　　　　　　　　　　　　　　　　　　　　　　　6._____
　　　 B. Howard Black
　　　 C. J. Howard Black
　　　 D. John H. Black

7.　　A. Theodora Garth Kingston　　　　　　　　　　　　　　　　　　　7._____
　　　 B. Theadore Barth Kingston
　　　 C. Thomas Kingston
　　　 D. Thomas T. Kingston

8.　　A. Paulette Mary Huerta　　　　　　　　　　　　　　　　　　　　8._____
　　　 B. Paul M. Huerta
　　　 C. Paulette L. Huerta
　　　 D. Peter A. Huerta

9. A. Martha Hunt Morgan   9.____
    B. Martin Hunt Morgan
    C. Mary H. Morgan
    D. Martine H. Morgan

10. A. James T. Meerschaum   10.____
    B. James M. Mershum
    C. James F. Mearshaum
    D. James N. Meshum

Questions 11-14.

DIRECTIONS: Questions 11 through 14 are to be answered SOLELY on the basis of the following information.

You are required to file various documents in file drawers which are labeled according to the following pattern:

DOCUMENTS

MEMOS		LETTERS	
File	Subject	File	Subject
84PM1 - (A-L)		84PC1 - (A-L)	
84PM2 - (M-Z)		84PC2 - (M-Z)	

REPORTS		INQUIRIES	
File	Subject	File	Subject
84PR1 - (A-L)		84PQ1 - (A-L)	
84PR2 - (M-Z)		84PQ2 - (M-Z)	

11. A letter dealing with a burglary should be filed in the drawer labeled   11.____

    A. 84PM1   B. 84PC1   C. 84PR1   D. 84PQ2

12. A report on Statistics should be found in the drawer labeled   12.____

    A. 84PM1   B. 84PC2   C. 84PR2   D. 84PQ2

13. An inquiry is received about parade permit procedures. It should be filed in the drawer   13.____
labeled

    A. 84PM2   B. 84PC1   C. 84PR1   D. 84PQ2

14. A police officer has a question about a robbery report you filed.   14.____
You should pull this file from the drawer labeled

    A. 84PM1   B. 84PM2   C. 84PR1   D. 84PR2

Questions 15-22.

DIRECTIONS: Each of Questions 15 through 22 consists of four or six numbered names. For each question, choose the option (A, B, C, or D) which indicates the order in which the names should be filed in accordance with the following filing instructions:
- File alphabetically according to last name, then first name, then middle initial.
- File according to each successive letter within a name.

- When comparing two names in which, the letters in the longer name are identical to the corresponding letters in the shorter name, the shorter name is filed first.
- When the last names are the same, initials are always filed before names beginning with the same letter.

15.   I.   Ralph Robinson   15.___
        II. Alfred Ross
        III. Luis Robles
        IV. James Roberts

The CORRECT filing sequence for the above names should be

A. IV, II, I, III   B. I, IV, III, II
C. III, IV, I, II   D. IV, I, III, II

16.   I.   Irwin Goodwin   16.___
        II. Inez Gonzalez
        III. Irene Goodman
        IV. Ira S. Goodwin
        V. Ruth I. Goldstein
        VI. M.B. Goodman

The CORRECT filing sequence for the above names should be

A. V, II, I, IV, III, VI   B. V, II, VI, III, IV, I
C. V, II, III, VI, IV, I   D. V, II, III, VI, I, IV

17.   I.   George Allan   17.___
        II. Gregory Allen
        III. Gary Allen
        IV. George Allen

The CORRECT filing sequence for the above names should be

A. IV, III, I, II   B. I, IV, II, III
C. III, IV, I, II   D. I, III, IV, II

18.   I.   Simon Kauffman   18.___
        II. Leo Kaufman
        III. Robert Kaufmann
        IV. Paul Kauffmann

The CORRECT filing sequence for the above names should be

A. I, IV, II, III   B. II, IV, III, I
C. III, II, IV, I   D. I, II, III, IV

19.   I.   Roberta Williams   19.___
        II. Robin Wilson
        III. Roberta Wilson
        IV. Robin Williams

The CORRECT filing sequence for the above names should be

A. III, II, IV, I   B. I, IV, III, II
C. I, II, III, IV   D. III, I, II, IV

20.
    I. Lawrence Shultz
    II. Albert Schultz
    III. Theodore Schwartz
    IV. Thomas Schwarz
    V. Alvin Schultz
    VI. Leonard Shultz

The CORRECT filing sequence for the above names should be

A. II, V, III, IV, I, VI   B. IV, III, V, I, II, VI
C. II, V, I, VI, III, IV   D. I, VI, II, V, III, IV

20.____

21.
    I. McArdle
    II. Mayer
    III. Maletz
    IV. McNiff
    V. Meyer
    VI. MacMahon

The CORRECT filing sequence for the above names should be

A. I, IV, VI, III, II, V   B. II, I, IV, VI, III, V
C. VI, III, II, I, IV, V   D. VI, III, II, V, I, IV

21.____

22.
    I. Jack E. Johnson
    II. R.H. Jackson
    III. Bertha Jackson
    IV. J.T. Johnson
    V. Ann Johns
    VI. John Jacobs

The CORRECT filing sequence for the above names should be

A. II, III, VI, V, IV, I   B. III, II, VI, V, IV, I
C. VI, II, III, I, V, IV   D. III, II, VI, IV, V, I

22.____

Questions 23-30.

DIRECTIONS: The code table below shows 10 letters with matching numbers. For each question, there are three sets of letters. Each set of letters is followed by a set of numbers which may or may not match their correct letter according to the code table. For each question, check all three sets of letters and numbers and mark your answer:
    A. if no pairs are correctly matched
    B. if only one pair is correctly matched
    C. if only two pairs are correctly matched
    D. if all three pairs are correctly matched

CODE TABLE

T	M	V	D	S	P	R	G	B	H
1	2	3	4	5	6	7	8	9	0

Sample Question: TMVDSP - 123456
    RGBHTM - 789011
    DSPRGB - 256789

In the sample question above, the first set of numbers correctly matches its set of letters. But the second and third pairs contain mistakes. In the second pair, M is incorrectly matched with number 1. According to the code table, letter M should be correctly matched with number 2. In the third pair, the letter D is incorrectly matched with number 2. According to the code table, letter D should be correctly matched with number 4. Since only one of the pairs is correctly matched, the answer to this sample question is B.

23. RSBMRM 759262
    GDSRVH 845730
    VDBRTM 349713
                                                                                      23.____

24. TGVSDR 183247
    SMHRDP 520647
    TRMHSR 172057
                                                                                     24.____

25. DSPRGM 456782
    MVDBHT 234902
    HPMDBT 062491
                                                                                    25.____

26. BVPTRD 936184
    GDPHMB 807029
    GMRHMV 827032
                                                                                    26.____

27. MGVRSH 283750
    TRDMBS 174295
    SPRMGV 567283
                                                                                    27.____

28. SGBSDM 489542
    MGHPTM 290612
    MPBMHT 269301
                                                                                    28.____

29. TDPBHM 146902
    VPBMRS 369275
    GDMBHM 842902
                                                                                    29.____

30. MVPTBV 236194
    PDRTMB 647128
    BGTMSM 981232
                                                                                    30.____

KEY (CORRECT ANSWERS)

1.	A	11.	B	21.	C
2.	C	12.	C	22.	B
3.	B	13.	D	23.	B
4.	D	14.	D	24.	B
5.	D	15.	D	25.	C
6.	B	16.	C	26.	A
7.	B	17.	D	27.	D
8.	B	18.	A	28.	A
9.	A	19.	B	29.	D
10.	C	20.	A	30.	A

TEST 2

Questions 1-10.

DIRECTIONS: Questions 1 through 10 each consists of two columns, each containing four lines of names, numbers and/or addresses. For each question, compare the lines in Column I with the lines in Column II to see if they match exactly, and mark your answer A, B, C, or D, according to the following instructions:
- A. all four lines match exactly
- B. only three lines match exactly
- C. only two lines match exactly
- D. only one line matches exactly

		COLUMN I	COLUMN II	
1.	I.	Earl Hodgson	Earl Hodgson	1.____
	II.	1409870	1408970	
	III.	Shore Ave.	Schore Ave.	
	IV.	Macon Rd.	Macon Rd.	
2.	I.	9671485	9671485	2.____
	II.	470 Astor Court	470 Astor Court	
	III.	Halprin, Phillip	Halperin, Phillip	
	IV.	Frank D. Poliseo	Frank D. Poliseo	
3.	I.	Tandem Associates	Tandom Associates	3.____
	II.	144-17 Northern Blvd.	144-17 Northern Blvd.	
	III.	Alberta Forchi	Albert Forchi	
	IV.	Kings Park, NY 10751	Kings Point, NY 10751	
4.	I.	Bertha C. McCormack	Bertha C. McCormack	4.____
	II.	Clayton, MO.	Clayton, MO.	
	III.	976-4242	976-4242	
	IV.	New City, NY 10951	New City, NY 10951	
5.	I.	George C. Morill	George C. Morrill	5.____
	II.	Columbia, SC 29201	Columbia, SD 29201	
	III.	Louis Ingham	Louis Ingham	
	IV.	3406 Forest Ave.	3406 Forest Ave.	
6.	I.	506 S. Elliott Pl.	506 S. Elliott Pl.	6.____
	II.	Herbert Hall	Hurbert Hall	
	III.	4712 Rockaway Pkway	4712 Rockaway Pkway	
	IV.	169 E. 7 St.	169 E. 7 St.	

	COLUMN I	COLUMN II	
7.	I. 345 Park Ave.	345 Park Pl.	7.____
	II. Colman Oven Corp.	Coleman Oven Corp.	
	III. Robert Conte	Robert Conti	
	IV. 6179846	6179846	

8.
    I. Grigori Schierber   Grigori Schierber   8.____
    II. Des Moines, Iowa   Des Moines, Iowa
    III. Gouverneur Hospital   Gouverneur Hospital
    IV. 91-35 Cresskill Pl.   91-35 Cresskill Pl.

9.
    I. Jeffery Janssen   Jeffrey Janssen   9.____
    II. 8041071   8041071
    III. 40 Rockefeller Plaza   40 Rockafeller Plaza
    IV. 407 6 St.   406 7 St.

10.
    I. 5971996   5871996   10.____
    II. 3113 Knickerbocker Ave.   3113 Knickerbocker Ave.
    III. 8434 Boston Post Rd.   8424 Boston Post Rd.
    IV. Penn Station   Penn Station

Questions 11-14.

DIRECTIONS: Questions 11 through 14 are to be answered by looking at the four groups of names and addresses listed below (I, II, III, and IV) and then finding out the number of groups that have their corresponding numbered lines exactly the same.

GROUP I
Line 1. Richmond General Hospital
Line 2. Geriatric Clinic
Line 3. 3975 Paerdegat St.
Line 4 Loudonville, New York 11538

GROUP II
Richman General Hospital
Geriatric Clinic
3975 Peardegat St.
Londonville, New York 11538

GROUP III
Line 1. Richmond General Hospital
Line 2. Geriatric Clinic
Line 3. 3795 Paerdegat St.
Line 4. Loudonville, New York 11358

GROUP IV
Richmend General Hospital
Geriatric Clinic
3975 Paerdegat St.
Loudonville, New York 11538

11. In how many groups is line one exactly the same?   11.____

    A. Two   B. Three   C. Four   D. None

12. In how many groups is line two exactly the same?   12.____

    A. Two   B. Three   C. Four   D. None

13. In how many groups is line three exactly the same?   13.____

    A. Two   B. Three   C. Four   D. None

14. In how many groups is line four exactly the same?   14.____

    A. Two   B. Three   C. Four   D. None

Questions 15-18.

DIRECTIONS: Each of Questions 15 through 18 has two lists of names and addresses. Each list contains three sets of names and addresses. Check each of the three sets in the list on the right to see if they are the same as the corresponding set in the list on the left. Mark your answers:
    A. if none of the sets in the right list are the same as those in the left list
    B. if only one of the sets in the right list is the same as those in the left list
    C. if only two of the sets in the right list are the same as those in the left list
    D. if all three sets in the right list are the same as those in the left list

15.
Mary T. Berlinger   Mary T. Berlinger   15.____
2351 Hampton St.   2351 Hampton St.
Monsey, N.Y. 20117   Monsey, N.Y. 20117

Eduardo Benes   Eduardo Benes
473 Kingston Avenue   473 Kingston Avenue
Central Islip, N.Y. 11734   Central Islip, N.Y. 11734

Alan Carrington Fuchs   Alan Carrington Fuchs
17 Gnarled Hollow Road   17 Gnarled Hollow Road
Los Angeles, CA 91635   Los Angeles, CA 91685

16.
David John Jacobson   David John Jacobson   16.____
178 35 St. Apt. 4C   178 53 St. Apt. 4C
New York, N.Y. 00927   New York, N.Y. 00927

Ann-Marie Calonella   Ann-Marie Calonella
7243 South Ridge Blvd.   7243 South Ridge Blvd.
Bakersfield, CA 96714   Bakersfield, CA 96714

Pauline M. Thompson   Pauline M. Thomson
872 Linden Ave.   872 Linden Ave.
Houston, Texas 70321   Houston, Texas 70321

17.
Chester LeRoy Masterton   Chester LeRoy Masterson   17.____
152 Lacy Rd.   152 Lacy Rd.
Kankakee, Ill. 54532   Kankakee, Ill. 54532

William Maloney   William Maloney
S. LaCrosse Pla.   S. LaCross Pla.
Wausau, Wisconsin 52146   Wausau, Wisconsin 52146

Cynthia V. Barnes   Cynthia V. Barnes
16 Pines Rd.   16 Pines Rd.
Greenpoint, Miss. 20376   Greenpoint, Miss. 20376

18.
Marcel Jean Frontenac
8 Burton On The Water
Calender, Me. 01471

J. Scott Marsden
174 S. Tipton St.
Cleveland, Ohio

Lawrence T. Haney
171 McDonough St.
Decatur, Ga. 31304

Marcel Jean Frontenac
6 Burton On The Water
Calender, Me. 01471

J. Scott Marsden
174 Tipton St.
Cleveland, Ohio

Lawrence T. Haney
171 McDonough St.
Decatur, Ga. 31304

18.____

Questions 19-26.

DIRECTIONS: Each of Questions 19 through 26 has two lists of numbers. Each list contains three sets of numbers. Check each of the three sets in the list on the right to see if they are the same as the corresponding set in the list on the left. Mark your answers:
A. if none of the sets in the right list are the same as those in the left list
B. if only one of the sets in the right list is the same as those in the left list
C. if only two of the sets in the right list are the same as those in the left list
D. if all three sets in the right list are the same as those in the left list

19. 7354183476
4474747744
57914302311

7354983476
4474747774
57914302311

19.____

20. 7143592185
8344517699
9178531263

7143892185
8344518699
9178531263

20.____

21. 2572114731
8806835476
8255831246

257214731
8806835476
8255831246

21.____

22. 331476853821
6976658532996
3766042113715

331476858621
6976655832996
3766042113745

22.____

23. 8806663315
74477138449
211756663666

8806663315
74477138449
211756663666

23.____

24. 990006966996
53022219743
4171171117717

99000696996
53022219843
4171171177717

24.____

25. 24400222433004
5300030055000355
20000075532002022

24400222433004
5300030055500355
20000075532002022

25.____

26. 611166640660001116   61116664066001116   26.____
     7111300117001100733   7111300117001100733
     26666446664476518   26666446664476518

Questions 27-30.

DIRECTIONS: Questions 27 through 30 are to be answered by picking the answer which is in
             the correct numerical order, from the lowest number to the highest number, in
             each question.

27. A. 44533, 44518, 44516, 44547   27.____
     B. 44516, 44518, 44533, 44547
     C. 44547, 44533, 44518, 44516
     D. 44518, 44516, 44547, 44533

28. A. 95587, 95593, 95601, 95620   28.____
     B. 95601, 95620, 95587, 95593
     C. 95593, 95587, 95601, 95620
     D. 95620, 95601, 95593, 95587

29. A. 232212, 232208, 232232, 232223   29.____
     B. 232208, 232223, 232212, 232232
     C. 232208, 232212, 232223, 232232
     D. 232223, 232232, 232208, 232212

30. A. 113419, 113521, 113462, 113588   30.____
     B. 113588, 113462, 113521, 113419
     C. 113521, 113588, 113419, 113462
     D. 113419, 113462, 113521, 113588

KEY (CORRECT ANSWERS)

1. C	11. A	21. C
2. B	12. C	22. A
3. D	13. A	23. D
4. A	14. A	24. A
5. C	15. C	25. C
6. B	16. B	26. C
7. D	17. B	27. B
8. A	18. B	28. A
9. D	19. B	29. C
10. C	20. B	30. D

NAME and NUMBER COMPARISONS

COMMENTARY

This test seeks to measure your ability and disposition to do a job carefully and accurately, your attention to exactness and preciseness of detail, your alertness and versatility in discerning similarities and differences between things, and your power in systematically handling written language symbols.

It is actually a test of your ability to do academic and/or clerical work, using the basic elements of verbal (qualitative) and mathematical (quantitative) learning – words and numbers.

EXAMINATION SECTION
TEST 1

Tests 1-2

DIRECTIONS: Questions 1 through 6 consist of sets of names and addresses. In each question, the name and address in Column II should be an exact copy of the name and address in Column I. *PRINT IN THE SPACE AT THE RIGHT THE LETTER:*
    A.   if there is a mistake only in the name
    B.   if there is a mistake only in the address
    C.   if there is a mistake in both name and address
    D.   if there is no mistake in either name or address

SAMPLE:

Michael Filbert   Michael Filbert
456 Reade Street   645 Reade Street
New York, N.Y. 10013   New York, N.Y. 10013

Since there is a mistake only in the address, the answer is B.

1.   Esta Wong   Esta Wang   1.____
      141 West 68 St.   141 West 68 St.
      New York, N.Y. 10023   New York, N.Y. 10023

2.   Dr. Alberto Grosso   Dr. Alberto Grosso   2.____
      3475 12th Avenue   3475 12th Avenue
      Brooklyn, N.Y. 11218   Brooklyn, N.Y. 11218

3.   Mrs. Ruth Bortlas   Ms. Ruth Bortlas   3.____
      482 Theresa Ct.   482 Theresa Ct.
      Far Rockaway, N.Y. 11691 Far Rockaway, N.Y. 11169

4.   Mr. and Mrs. Howard Fox Mr. and Mrs. Howard Fox 4.____
      2301 Sedgwick Ave.   231 Sedgwick Ave.
      Bronx, N.Y. 10468   Bronx, N.Y. 10468

5.   Miss Marjorie Black   Miss Margorie Black   5.____
      223 East 23 Street   223 East 23 Street
      New York, N.Y. 10010   New York, N.Y. 10010

6. Michelle Herman
    806 Valley Rd.
    Old Tappan, N.J. 07675

Michelle Hermann
806 Valley Dr.
Old Tappan, N.J. 07675

6.____

KEY (CORRECT ANSWERS)

1. A
2. D
3. C
4. B
5. A
6. C

TEST 2

DIRECTIONS: Questions 1 through 6 consist of sets of names and addresses. In each question, the name and address in Column II should be an exact copy of the name and address in Column I. *PRINT IN THE SPACE AT THE RIGHT THE LETTER:*

    A. if there is a mistake only in the name
    B. if there is a mistake only in the address
    C. if there is a mistake in both name and address
    D. if there is no mistake in either name or address

1. Ms. Joan Kelly
   313 Franklin Ave.
   Brooklyn, N.Y. 11202

   Ms. Joan Kielly
   318 Franklin Ave.
   Brooklyn, N.Y. 11202

   1._____

2. Mrs. Eileen Engel
   47-24 86 Road
   Queens, N.Y. 11122

   Mrs. Ellen Engel
   47-24 86 Road
   Queens, N.Y. 11122

   2._____

3. Marcia Michaels
   213 E. 81 St.
   New York, N.Y. 10012

   Marcia Michaels
   213 E. 81 St.
   New York, N.Y. 10012

   3._____

4. Rev. Edward J. Smyth
   1401 Brandeis Street
   San Francisco, Calif. 96201

   Rev. Edward J. Smyth
   1401 Brandies Street
   San Francisco, Calif. 96201

   4._____

5. Alicia Rodriguez
   24-68 81 St.
   Elmhurst, N.Y. 11122

   Alicia Rodriquez
   2468 81 St.
   Elmhurst, N.Y. 11122

   5._____

6. Ernest Eisemann
   21 Columbia St.
   New York, N.Y. 10007

   Ernest Eisermann
   21 Columbia St.
   New York, N.Y. 10007

   6._____

KEY (CORRECT ANSWERS)

1. C
2. A
3. D
4. B
5. C
6. A

TEST 3

DIRECTIONS: Questions 1 through 8 consist of names, locations and telephone numbers. In each question, the name, location and number in Column II should be an exact copy of the name, location and number in Column I. *PRINT IN THE SPACE AT THE RIGHT THE LETTER:*
- A. if there is a mistake in one line only
- B. if there is a mistake in two lines only
- C. if there is a mistake in three lines only
- D. if there are no mistakes in any of the lines

1. Ruth Lang
EAM Bldg., Room C101
625-2000, ext. 765

   Ruth Lang
   EAM Bldg., Room C110
   625-2000, ext. 765

   1._____

2. Anne Marie Ionozzi
Investigations, Room 827
576-4000, ext. 832

   Anna Marie Ionozzi
   Investigation, Room 827
   566-4000, ext. 832

   2._____

3. Willard Jameson
Fm C Bldg. Room 687
454-3010

   Willard Jamieson
   Fm C Bldg. Room 687
   454-3010

   3._____

4. Joanne Zimmermann
Bldg. SW, Room 314
532-4601

   Joanne Zimmermann
   Bldg. SW, Room 314
   532-4601

   4._____

5. Carlyle Whetstone
Payroll Division-A, Room 212A
262-5000, ext. 471

   Caryle Whetstone
   Payroll Division-A, Room 212A
   262-5000, ext. 417

   5._____

6. Kenneth Chiang
Legal Council, Room 9745
(201) 416-9100, ext. 17

   Kenneth Chiang
   Legal Counsel, Room 9745
   (201) 416-9100, ext. 17

   6._____

7. Ethel Koenig
Personnel Services Div, Rm 433
635-7572

   Ethel Hoenig
   Personal Services Div, Rm 433
   635-7527

   7._____

8. Joyce Ehrhardt
Office of Administrator, Rm W56
387-8706

   Joyce Ehrhart
   Office of Administrator, Rm W56
   387-7806

   8._____

KEY (CORRECT ANSWERS)

1. A
2. C
3. A
4. D
5. B

6. A
7. C
8. B

———

TEST 4

DIRECTIONS: Each of questions 1 through 10 gives the identification number and name of a person who has received treatment at a certain hospital. You are to choose the option (A, B, C or D) which has EXACTLY the same number and name as those given in the question.

SAMPLE:
123765 Frank Y. Jones
- A. 123675 Frank Y. Jones
- B. 123765 Frank T. Jones
- C. 123765 Frank Y. Johns
- D. 123765 Frank Y. Jones

The correct answer is D, because it is the only option showing the identification number and name exactly as they are in the sample question.

1. 754898 Diane Malloy

    1.___

    - A. 745898 Diane Malloy
    - B. 754898 Dion Malloy
    - C. 754898 Diane Malloy
    - D. 754898 Diane Maloy

2. 661818 Ferdinand Figueroa

    2.___

    - A. 661818 Ferdinand Figeuroa
    - B. 661618 Ferdinand Figueroa
    - C. 661818 Ferdnand Figueroa
    - D. 661818 Ferdinand Figueroa

3. 100101 Norman D. Braustein

    3.___

    - A. 100101 Norman D. Braustein
    - B. 101001 Norman D. Braustein
    - C. 100101 Norman P. Braustien
    - D. 100101 Norman D. Bruastein

4. 838696 Robert Kittredge

    4.___

    - A. 838969 Robert Kittredge
    - B. 838696 Robert Kittredge
    - C. 388696 Robert Kittredge
    - D. 838696 Robert Kittridge

5. 243716 Abraham Soletsky

    5.___

    - A. 243716 Abrahm Soletsky
    - B. 243716 Abraham Solestky
    - C. 243176 Abraham Soletsky
    - D. 243716 Abraham Soletsky

6. 981121 Phillip M. Maas   6.____

    A. 981121 Phillip M. Mass
    B. 981211 Phillip M. Maas
    C. 981121 Phillip M. Maas
    D. 981121 Phillip N. Maas

7. 786556 George Macalusso   7.____

    A. 785656 George Macalusso
    B. 786556 George Macalusso
    C. 786556 George Maculusso
    D. 786556 George Macluasso

8. 639472 Eugene Weber   8.____

    A. 639472 Eugene Weber
    B. 639472 Eugene Webre
    C. 693472 Eugene Weber
    D. 639742 Eugene Weber

9. 724936 John J. Lomonaco   9.____

    A. 724936 John J. Lomanoco
    B. 724396 John L. Lomonaco
    C. 724936 John J. Lomonaco
    D. 724936 John J. Lamonaco

10. 899868 Michael Schnitzer   10.____

    A. 899868 Micheal Schnitzer
    B. 898968 Michael Schnizter
    C. 899688 Michael Schnitzer
    D. 899868 Michael Schnitzer

KEY (CORRECT ANSWERS)

1.	C	6.	C
2.	D	7.	B
3.	A	8.	A
4.	B	9.	C
5.	D	10.	D

NAME AND NUMBER CHECKING
EXAMINATION SECTION
TEST 1

DIRECTIONS: Each question consists of a name, address, and social security number, arranged in 2 lists. List I is correct, but some mistakes were made in copying the information to List II. For each question, you must check to see if there are any mistakes in List II. Mark your answer A if there are no mistakes in List II. Mark your answer B if there is a mistake in List II.

LIST I	LIST II	
1. BRUCE CHAMBERS 211 MIAMI ROAD 879-86-3417	Bruce Chambers 211 Miami Blvd. 879-86-3417	1._____
2. PAUL NEADERLANDER 2 CIRCLE DRIVE 294-04-7199	Paul Neaderlander 2 Circle Drive 294-04-7199	2._____
3. ERNESTINE THOMPSON 87 WEST 9TH STREET 949-09-7211	Ernestine Thompson 87 West 9th Street 949-09-7211	3._____
4. JOANNE MYERS 16 TOPPLETREE ROAD 655-29-0733	Joanne Meyers 16 Toppletree Road 655-29-0733	4._____
5. EMILY JONES 40 HADLEY AVENUE 269-79-0011	Emily Jones 40 Hadley Avenue 269-09-0011	5._____
6. FRANKLIN GRETSKY 99 DOLPHIN AVENUE 879-09-2111	Franklin Geretsky 99 Dolphin Avenue 879-09-2111	6._____
7. BARBERA EVANS 16 BARNABY LANE 269-04-7711	Barbara Evans 16 Barnaby Lane 269-04-7711	7._____
8. RICHARD BELTZER 119 MONTAGUE STREET 079-29-0473	Richard Beltzer 119 Montague Street 079-29-0473	8._____
9. LEE TEMPLE 498 EAST 16TH N.W. 249-07-3711	Lee Temple 498 East 61st N.W. 249-07-3711	9._____
10. MADELINE DOUGHERTY 330 TIMBERLANE ROAD 269-04-7712	Madeline Dougherty 330 Timberlane Road 269-04-7712	10._____

LIST I	LIST II	
11. PETULIA FOX 16 MANN TERRACE 749-09-2911	Petulia Fox 16 Mann Terrace 749-09-0911	11.____
12. MARION ROLLINS 279 MANOR ROAD 478-86-2711	Marion Rollins 279 Manor Road 478-86-2711	12.____
13. ROBERTA JACKSON 2 PAINTERS LANE 876-27-9449	Roberta Jackson 2 Printers Lane 876-27-9449	13.____
14. LYNN PURCELL 1681 FORD ROAD 279-09-8733	Lynn Purcell 1681 Ford Road 279-09-8733	14.____
15. MANNY EISEN 27-11 OCEAN BLVD. 879-21-4711	Manny Eisen 27-11 Ocean Blvd. 879-21-4711	15.____
16. MARK HANOVER 47 TULIP LANE 279-08-0771	Mark Hanover 47 Tulip Lane 279-08-0771	16.____
17. MARIANNE MATTHEWS 81 RIVERSIDE DRIVE 871-29-4211	Marianne Matthews 81 Riverside Drive 871-29-4211	17.____
18. CHARLES DOUGLAS 27 MONTGOMERY ROAD 879-29-4011	Charles Douglas 27 Montgomry Road 879-29-4011	18.____
19. LONNY DONALDSON 87 PETERS AVENUE 277-63-0739	Lonny Donaldson 87 Peters Avenue 277-63-0739	19.____
20. PATRICK MCCOLLOUGH 168 BARRON STREET 899-26-4733	Patrick McCollough 168 Barron Street 899-26-4733	20.____
21. JOHN ALEXANDER 425 WEST END AVENUE 876-01-2371	John Alexanders 425 West End Avenue 876-01-2371	21.____
22. PHILIP MANCHESTER 86 GIBBONS DRIVE 297-83-0124	Philip Manchester 86 Gibbons Drive 297-38-0124	22.____
23. ALYSSIA SARKOV 1086A ELM STREET 249-66-0371	Alyssia Sarkov 1086A Elm Street 249-66-0371	23.____

3 (#1)

LIST I   LIST II

24. TREMONT KLEE   Tremont Klee   24.____
     9272 YORKVILLE ROAD   9272 Yorkville Road
     265-54-2793   265-54-2973

25. EVAN FISCH   Evan Fisch   25.____
     824 BELLOWS LANE   842 Bellows Lane
     244-78-0733   244-78-0733

_____

KEY (CORRECT ANSWERS)

1. B   211 Miami <u>Blvd.</u>
2. A
3. A
4. B   M<u>e</u>yers
5. B   269-<u>09</u>-0011

6. B   G<u>e</u>retsky
7. B   Barb<u>a</u>ra
8. A
9. B   498 East <u>61</u>st Street
10. A

11. B   749-09-<u>0</u>911
12. A
13. B   2 P<u>r</u>inters Lane
14. A
15. A

16. A
17. A
18. B   27 Montgo<u>mr</u>y Road
19. A
20. A

21. B   Alexander<u>s</u>
22. B   297-<u>38</u>-0124
23. A
24. B   265-54-2<u>97</u>3
25. B   8<u>42</u> Bellows Lane

_____

169

TEST 2

DIRECTIONS: Each question consists of a name, address, and social security number, arranged in 2 lists. List I is correct, but some mistakes were made in copying the information to List II. For each question, you must check to see if there are any mistakes in List II. Mark your answer A if there are no mistakes in List II. Mark your answer B if there is a mistake in List II.

LIST I   LIST II

1. CONNIE SISKIN   Connie Siskin   1.____
    4 ELIZABETH LANE   4 Elizabeth Lane
    679-24-2211   679-24-2211

2. YOLANDA PRINCIPE   Yolanda Principe   2.____
    19 FORREST STREET   19 Forest Street
    876-24-6711   876-24-6711

3. MADELINE PHILLIPS   Madeline Phillips   3.____
    16 STONEY POINT ROAD   16 Stoney Point Road
    279-24-0779   279-24-0799

4. OSVALDO SOUZA   Osvaldo Souza   4.____
    1681 YORK AVENUE   1681 York Avenue
    678-23-4271   678-23-4271

5. CATHERINE ELLISON   Catharine Ellison   5.____
    4248TH AVENUE S.W.   4248th Avenue S.W.
    269-72-7388   269-72-7388

6. FRANKLIN AQUINO   Franklin Aquino   6.____
    827 RYDERS LANE   827 Ryders Lane
    777-01-2455   777-01-2455

7. STEPHANIE FOREMAN   Stepfanie Foreman   7.____
    1096 FEDERAL CIRCLE   1096 Federal Circle
    287-79-0334   287-79-0334

8. MICHAEL O'NEILL   Michael O'Neil   8.____
    16 FLORENCE ROAD   16 Florence Road
    989-76-7661   989-76-7661

9. SANDRA MORRIS   Sandra Morris   9.____
    16 BELMONT AVENUE   16 Belmont Avenue
    248-16-7111   248-16-1711

10. FRANCIS MURRAY   Francis Murray   10.____
    2 TARKINGTON AVENUE   2 Tarkington Avenue
    755-81-1211   755-81-1211

11. ADRIAN GOLDSTEIN   Adrien Goldstein   11.____
    14 CIRCLE DRIVE NORTH   14 Circle Drive North
    798-81-2171   798-81-2171

LIST I	LIST II	
12. PHYLICIA FOXX 191 MYERS ROAD 678-01-2371	Phylicia Foxx 191 Myers Road 678-01-2371	12.____
13. MARION NORDSTROM 249 WEST 86TH STREET 279-49-0711	Marion Nordstrom 249 West 86th Street 249-79-0711	13.____
14. RONALD PLOTTSKIN 2 AMELIA AVENUE 544-36-0781	Ronald Plottkin 2 Amelia Avenue 544-36-0781	14.____
15. WILLIAM DWYER 21 MIDDLE STREET 876-81-8112	William Dwyer 21 Middle Street 876-18-8112	15.____
16. PETER FILMORE 788 PARK LANE 799-23-0142	Peter Filmore 788 Park Lane 789-23-0142	16.____
17. KAREN STANISLAVSKY 498 TERMINAL ACCESS ROAD 611-27-4111	Karen Stanislawsky 498 Terminal Access Road 611-27-4111	17.____
18. EDWARD PUSHKIN 67-89 MAPLE STREET 278-86-7899	Edward Pushkin 67-89 Maple Street 278-68-7899	18.____
19. CHRISTINA FABRIKANT 116 EAST 111TH STREET 249-09-7381	Christine Fabrikant 116 East 111th Street 249-09-7381	19.____
20. CHARLES KLEINMAN 1061 MADISON AVENUE 354-86-1102	Charles Kleinman 1061 Madison Avenue 354-86-1102	20.____
21. DOMINIC LACATA 33 GREENWICH AVENUE 274-86-0311	Dominic Lacata 33 Greenich Avenue 274-86-0311	21.____
22. PAUL LEVY 1086A 20TH STREET 102-80-0116	Paul Levy 1086A 20th Street 102-80-0116	22.____
23. PATRICIA MEADE 141 Cabrini Blvd. 689-37-2371	Patricia Meade 141 Cabrinni Blvd. 689-37-2371	23.____
24. MORRIS FELINSKY 9 PRUDENCE PLACE 789-36-2499	Morris Felinsky 9 Prudence Place 789-63-2499	24.____

	LIST I	LIST II	

25. ESTER PRADO
17 EAST 16TH STREET
246-03-0919

Ester Prado
17 East 15th Street
246-03-0919

25.____

26. BARBARA POWELL
75 MONTGOMERY ROAD
879-23-6754

Barbara Powell
75 Montgomery Road
879-32-6754

26.____

27. RALPH BELLACCIO
269 WEST 76TH STREET
268-89-9442

Ralph Bellaccio
269 West 76th Street
269-89-9442

27.____

28. DENISE DAVIS
100 MORNINGSIDE DRIVE
249-29-6602

Denise Davis
100 Morningside Drive
249-29-6602

28.____

29. ANGELA TORRES
48 CHRISTOPHER STREET
649-09-2366

Angela Torres
48 Christopher Street
649-09-2366

29.____

30. LOUISE CHAPMAN
16 HATFIELD ROAD
682-66-5432

Louise Chapman
16 Hatfield Road
682-66-5342

30.____

————————

KEY (CORRECT ANSWERS)

1. A
2. B   19 Forest Street
3. B   279-24-0799
4. A
5. B   Catharine

6. A
7. B   Stepfanie
8. B   O'Neil_
9. B   248-16-1711
10. A

11. B   Adrien
12. A
13. B   249-79-0711
14. B   Plottkin
15. B   876-18-8112

16. B   789-23-0142
17. B   Stanislawsky
18. B   278-68-7899
19. B   Christine
20. A

21. B   33 Greenich Avenue
22. A
23. B   Cabrinni
24. B   789-63-2499
25. B   17 East 15th Street

26. B   879-32-6754
27. B   269-89-9442
28. A
29. A
30. B   682-66-5342

TEST 3

DIRECTIONS: Each question consists of a name, address, and social security number, arranged in 2 lists. List I is correct, but some mistakes were made in copying the information to List II. For each question, you must check to see if there are any mistakes in List II. Mark your answer A if there are no mistakes in List II. Mark your answer B if there is a mistake in List II.

<u>LIST I</u>   <u>LIST II</u>

1. HATTIE BERKER   Hattie Berker   1.____
    109-49 40TH STREET N.W.   109-49 40th Street N.W.
    268-38-4211   268-38-4211

2. MANUEL FELICIAS   Manuel Felicias   2.____
    2938 CANADA BLVD.   2968 Canada Blvd.
    168-33-9742   168-33-9742

3. BURTON BALANOWSKI   Burton Balanowski   3.____
    76 HADLEY BLVD.   76 Hadley Blvd.
    286-49-2311   286-49-3211

4. DAVID CONKLIN   David Conklin   4.____
    298 HOBOKEN STREET   298 Hoboken Street
    168-28-3798   168-28-3798

5. MICHELLE ROGET   Michele Roget   5.____
    10 AGAWAM ROAD   10 Agawam Road
    279-39-3722   279-39-3722

6. HANNA GREENE   Hanna Greene   6.____
    141 WEST 9TH STREET   141 West 9th Street
    876-36-3611   876-36-3611

7. BARRY NEWMARK   Barry Newmark   7.____
    42 TODD STREET   42 Todd Street
    867-32-7399   867-23-7399

8. MELISSA FEUTREL   Melissa Feutrel   8.____
    898 HERALD SQUARE   898 Herald Square
    267-79-2388   276-79-2388

9. AMY KINGSLEY   Amy Kingsely   9.____
    428 TOWNSHIP LANE   428 Township Lane
    771-17-2377   771-17-2377

10. PAMELA WINCHESTER   Pamela Winchester   10.____
    1781 DELUTH AVENUE   178 Deluth Avenue
    876-18-2733   876-18-2733

11. HORACE BUELOW   Horace Buelow   11.____
    1683 YORK STREET S.W.   1863 York Street S.W.
    478-09-7332   478-09-7332

LIST I | LIST II

12. ANNA MARIA BARDONNA
11 MAGENTA ROAD
679-23-0734

Anna Maria Bardonna
11 Margenta Road
679-23-0734

12.____

13. CECIL PAXTON
61 EAST 93RD STREET
679-03-4992

Cecil Paxton
61 East 93rd Street
678-03-4992

13.____

14. TAUREAN SIMPSON
1429-89 111TH STREET N.W.
479-83-7655

Taurean Simpson
1429-81 111th Street N.W.
479-83-7655

14.____

15. KATHY KETCHUM
4711 GRANT STREET
879-23-3754

Kathy Ketchum
40711 Grand Street
879-23-3754

15.____

16. JANET SCHAEFFER
27 CALDWELL AVENUE
683-23-7249

Janet Schaffer
27 Caldwell Avenue
683-23-7249

16.____

17. JAMES COBALT
25 CENTER CITY PARK
223-83-4947

James Cobalt
25 Center City Park
223-83-4749

17.____

18. CONNIE KELINSKI
97 CONKLIN STREET
776-25-9631

Connie Kelinski
97 Conklin Street
776-25-9631

18.____

19. HENRY ROUSSEAU
2 SIENNA DRIVE
777-07-2399

Henry Rousseau
2 Sienna Drive
777-07-2399

19.____

20. PETER MARKHAM
421 RYAN ROAD
687-37-4381

Peter Markham
412 Ryan Road
687-37-4381

20.____

21. WILLIAM JAMES
4798 BOSTON HWY.
679-23-4755

William Janes
4798 Boston Hwy.
679-23-4755

21.____

22. EDWARD STRUTTHERS
1611-27 UNION STREET
722-29-4785

Edward Struthers
1611-27 Union Street
722-29-4785

22.____

23. HANNA ROSENBLATT
798 COMMERCE STREET
211-01-0733

Hanna Rosenblatt
798 Commerce Street
211-01-0733

23.____

24. BEVERLY KINGSLEY
23 LAMBERT ROAD
429-79-3337

Beverly Kingsley
23 Lambert Road
429-73-3337

24.____

	LIST I	LIST II	
			24.____
25.	TIMOTHY TEMPKIN 334 E. 93RD STREET 233-09-4555	Timothy Tempkin 334 E. 93rd Street 233-09-4555	25.____
26.	GERALD MANN 16 LEXINGTON COURT 147-12-1612	Gerald Mann 16 Lexington Court 147-12-1216	26.____
27.	ANN KELLEHER 355 GREENFIELD AVENUE 298-47-2316	Ann Kelleher 355 Greenfield Avenue 298-47-2316	27.____
28.	GORDON CRAIG 1019 125TH STREET 883-23-0941	Gordon Craig 1019 135th Street 883-23-0941	28.____
29.	LEONARD SWEET 217 WEST 72ND STREET 244-45-2311	Leonard Sweet 217 West 72nd Street 244-54-2311	29.____
30.	SARAH FREIDLANDER 761 BENSONHURST AVENUE 551-12-2981	Sarah Freidlander 761 Bensonhurst Avenue 551-12-2981	30.____

———

KEY (CORRECT ANSWERS)

1. A
2. B   29<u>6</u>8 Canada Blvd.
3. B   286-49-<u>32</u>11
4. A
5. B   Miche<u>le</u>

6. A
7. B   867-<u>23</u>-7399
8. B   <u>276</u>-79-2388
9. B   Kingsely
10. B   178<u>1</u> Deluth Avenue

11. B   1<u>86</u>3 York Street S.W.
12. B   11 Ma<u>r</u>genta Road
13. B   67<u>8</u>-03-4992
14. B   1429-8<u>1</u>-111th Street
15. B   4711 Gran<u>d</u> Street

16. B   Scha<u>ff</u>er
17. B   223-83-4<u>74</u>9
18. A
19. A
20. B   4<u>12</u> Ryan Road

21. B   Ja<u>n</u>es
22. B   Str<u>ut</u>hers
23. A
24. B   429-7<u>3</u>-3337
25. A

26. B   147-12-1<u>21</u>6
27. A
28. B   1019 1<u>3</u>5th Street
29. B   244-<u>54</u>-2311
30. A
